HARDEN'S

Good Cheap Eats

in London 1999

mail@hardens.com
If you wish to send us any comments about this guide, or any of the places reviewed in it, you may find it convenient to do so by e-mail, to the above address.

© Harden's Guides, 1999

ISBN 1-873721-21-8

British Library Cataloguing-in-Publication data:
a catalogue record for this book is available from the British Library.

Printed and bound in Finland by
Werner Söderström Osakeyhtiö

Research and editorial assistants: Antonia Russell, Victoria Alers-Hankey

Harden's Guides
14 Buckingham Street
London WC2N 6DF

Distributed in the United States of America by
Seven Hills Book Distributors,
49 Central Avenue, Cincinnati, OH 45202

The contents of this book are believed correct at the time of printing. Nevertheless, the publishers can accept no responsibility for errors or changes in or omissions from the details given.

No part of this publication may be reproduced or transmitted in any form or by any means, electronically or mechanically, including photocopying, recording or any information storage or retrieval system, without

CONTENTS

Ratings & prices

	Page
Introduction	8

Recommendations

Top food – £15 a head or less	10
Top food – over £15 a head	10
Most interesting ethnic places	11
Special deals at top restaurants	11
Tops for romance	11
The best fun places	12
The most stylish places	12

Directory	14

Indexes

Breakfast	106
BYO	106
Children	107
Entertainment	108
Late	109
No-smoking areas	110
Outside tables	111
Pre/Post theatre	113
Private rooms	113
Vegetarian menus	114

Cuisine indexes	118
Area overviews	128
Maps	144

1 – London overview
2 – West End overview
3 – Mayfair, St James's & West Soho
4 – East Soho, Chinatown & Covent Garden
5 – Knightsbridge, Chelsea & South Kensington
6 – Notting Hill & Bayswater
7 – Hammersmith & Chiswick
8 – Hampstead, Camden Town & Islington
9 – The City
10 – South London (and Fulham)

RATINGS & PRICES

RATINGS

Ratings are based both on our own experiences – we have visited all of the establishments at our own expense – and also on the views of the reporters who take part in our annual survey. We have given ratings as follows:

★★ **Exceptional**
London's top bargains. They offer a quality of cooking which is, given the price, worth travelling for.

★ **Very good**
Places where the cooking offers above-average value for money.

𝔸 **Good atmosphere**
Spots with particular "buzz", style or charm.

PRICES

So you can compare the costs of different establishments, we have tried to give a realistic estimate of the cost for a typical meal in each place.

For *restaurants, pubs and wine bars,* we have given an estimate of the cost for one (1) person of two courses with a drink and a cup of coffee.

For *cafés,* the price we show is the approximate cost of a sandwich, a cake and a cup of coffee.

These prices include service (we have included a 10% tip if there is no service charge), VAT and any cover charge.

* Where an asterisk appears next to the price, you can usually keep expenditure to £20 a head or less only at certain times of day (usually lunch) or by sticking to a particular menu. Eating at other times or from the à la carte menu may be much more expensive – see the text of the entry for details. In the area lists, the ratings for such restaurants appear in brackets, eg (𝔸★).

Map reference – shown immediately after the telephone number.

Last orders time – the first entry in the small print (Sunday may be up to 90 minutes earlier).

Opening hours – unless otherwise stated, restaurants are open for lunch and dinner seven days a week.

Credit and debit cards – unless otherwise stated, Mastercard, Visa, Amex and Switch are accepted.

Smoking – cigarette smoking restrictions are noted. Pipe or cigar smokers should always check ahead.

INTRODUCTION

This is the fifth edition of our guide for anyone who wants to enjoy eating out in London while keeping costs under control. It is more possible than many people might think to find interesting and satisfying meals at modest cost. And it's not even as if you are restricted to a particular *type* of establishment. The coverage of this guide extends all the way from basic East End canteens to grand, 'big name' restaurants in the heart of fashionable London

We have decided to keep the same £20 a head "cut-off" price as we used for the last edition. For this amount, a qualifying establishment must provide two courses, a drink, coffee and service. (If there is no compulsory service charge, we have allowed for a 10% tip.) Many of the places listed can be visited for light meals or snacks at rather less cost than the "formula" price we quote.

Diners on a budget, in particular, have to know *where* to go, of course – but it's often almost more important to know *when*. Many of the more interesting experiences are to be had at places where the price is asterisked* – see the previous page for an explanation. These are usually "proper" restaurants which experience a shortage of custom at lunchtime (or, in some office areas, dinner time). They offer low-price set menus as loss leaders, hoping either to make up the difference through wine sales or to impress customers enough to guarantee a return visit. Whatever the restaurateurs' motives, there are some great bargains to be had – especially for those who do not need too much wine with their meal!

We wish you some excellent lunching and dining. Perhaps you would like to tell us about your successes (or any failures). Every summer, we conduct a detailed survey of the experiences of London restaurant-goers. Those who participate – over 3,400 people in 1998 – receive a complimentary copy of our comprehensive annual guide, *Harden's London Restaurants*, the following October.

We invite you, too, to take part in the survey. Just send us your name and address (or register by e-mail with mail@hardens.com), and you will be sent a form the following May, with a free update about major new restaurants (budget and not) which have opened over the previous few months.

Richard Harden **Peter Harden**

RECOMMENDATIONS

RECOMMENDATIONS

Top food

For £15 a head or less

Alounak *(W14)*
Beyoglu *(SW11)*
Brilliant *(UB2)*
Faulkner's *(E8)*
Fryer's Delight *(WC1)*
Kastoori *(SW17)*
Lahore Kebab House *(E1)*
Lisboa Patisserie *(W10)*
Lou Pescadou *(SW5)*
Luigi's Delicatessen *(SW10)*
Mon Plaisir *(WC2)*
Pizzeria Franco *(SW9)*
Ranoush *(W1)*
Seashell *(NW1)*
Shree Krishna *(SW17)*
Topsy-Tasty *(W4)*

For over £15 a head

Antipasto & Pasta *(SW11)*
The Apprentice *(SE1)*
Babur Brasserie *(SE23)*
Chelsea Ram *(SW10)*
Chez Liline *(N4)*
Chiswick Restaurant *(W4)*
Cibo *(W14)*
Eco *(SW4)*
The Gate *(W6)*
Gresslin's *(NW3)*
Hunan *(SW1)*
Inaho *(W2)*
Iznik *(N5)*
Launceston Place *(W8)*
Laurent *(NW2)*
Ma Goa *(SW15)*
Mandarin Kitchen *(W2)*
Mirabelle *(W1)*
Nine Golden Square *(W1)*
Odette's *(NW1)*
Le P'tit Normand *(SW18)*
Pizza Metro *(SW11)*
Popeseye *(W14)*
La Poule au Pot *(SW1)*
Ransome's Dock *(SW11)*
Rasa *(chain)*
Roussillon *(SW1)*
Royal China *(chain)*
Soho Spice *(W1)*
The Stepping Stone *(SW8)*
Toff's *(N10)*
Two Brothers *(N3)*
Veeraswamy *(W1)*

Most interesting ethnic places

Alounak (W14)
Babur Brasserie (SE23)
Beyoglu (SW11)
Brilliant (UB2)
Chez Liline (N4)
Chiang Mai (W1)
Esarn Kheaw (W12)
Hunan (SW1)
Ikkyu (chain)
Inaho (W2)
Iznik (N5)
Kastoori (SW17)
Lahore Kebab House (E1)
Laurent (NW2)
Ma Goa (SW15)
Mandarin Kitchen (W2)
Poons, Lisle Street (WC2)
Ranoush (W1)
Rasa (chain)
Royal China (chain)
Shree Krishna (SW17)
Soho Spice (W1)
Topsy-Tasty (W4)

Special deals at top restaurants

Bank (WC2)
Bluebird (SW3)
Butlers Wharf Chop-house (SE1)
Chutney Mary (SW10)
Cibo (W14)
Frederick's (N1)
Granita (N1)
Launceston Place (W8)
Lou Pescadou (SW5)
Matsuri (SW1)
Mirabelle (W1)
Momo (W1)
Mon Plaisir (WC2)
Monsieur Max (TW12)
Odette's (NW1)
Pasha (SW7)
Le Pont de la Tour Bar & Grill (SE1)
La Poule au Pot (SW1)
Ransome's Dock (SW11)
The Terrace (W8)
Veeraswamy (W1)

Tops for romance

Andrew Edmunds (W1)
Anglo Asian Tandoori (N16)
Arancia (SE16)
Aurora (W1)
Boudin Blanc (W1)
Brass. du Marché (W10)
The Fox Reformed (N16)
Frederick's (N1)
Frocks (E9)
Gordon's Wine Bar (WC2)
Iznik (N5)
Launceston Place (W8)
Mirabelle (W1)
Momo (W1)
Mon Plaisir (WC2)
Odette's (NW1)
Osteria Basilico (W11)
La Poule au Pot (SW1)
Sarastro (WC2)
The Stable (SW3)
The Terrace (W8)
Yum Yum (N16)

RECOMMENDATIONS

The best fun places

Alphabet (W1)
Balans (chain)
Bar Gansa (NW1)
Bar Italia (W1)
Benihana (chain)
Blues (W1)
Buona Sera (SW11)
Café Bohème (W1)
Café Emm (W1)
Café Latino (W1)
Cantaloupe (EC2)
don Fernando's (TW9)
don Pepe (NW8)
Eco (SW4)
Efes Kebab House (chain)
La Finca (chain)
Florians (N8)
El Gaucho (SW3)
Gordon's Wine Bar (WC2)
Hard Rock Café (W1)
Khan's (W2)
Lemonia (NW1)
Luigi's Delicatessen (SW10)
Mediterraneo (W11)
Meson Don Felipe (SE1)
Momo (W1)
Ost. Antica Bologna (SW11)
Osteria Basilico (W11)
Patio (W12)
Paulo's (W6)
La Piragua (N1)
Pizza Pomodoro (SW3)
Pizzeria Castello (SE1)
La Porchetta Pizzeria (N4)
Pucci Pizza (SW3)
Rebato's (SW8)
RK Stanleys (W1)
La Rueda (SW4)
Sarastro (WC2)
The Ship (SW18)
Sticky Fingers (W8)
The Sun & Doves (SE5)
Vingt-Quatre (SW10)
Wagamama (chain)
The Westbourne (W2)
Wong Kei (W1)
Yo! Sushi (W1)
Yum Yum (N16)
Zamoyski (NW3)

The most stylish places

The Abingdon (W8)
Aquarium (E1)
Bank (WC2)
Benihana (chain)
Bluebird (SW3)
Blues (W1)
Butlers Wharf
   Chop-house (SE1)
Café Bohème (W1)
Carnevale (EC1)
The Crescent (SW3)
La Delizia (chain)
East One (EC1)
Eco (SW4)
Frederick's (N1)
Granita (N1)
Gung-Ho (NW6)
Home (EC1)
Lansdowne (NW1)
Launceston Place (W8)
Mango Room (NW1)
Mirabelle (W1)
Momo (W1)
Odette's (NW1)
Pasha (SW7)
Pizza On The Park (SW1)
PizzaExpress (chain)
Pizzeria Condotti (W1)
Le Pont de la Tour Bar
   & Grill (SE1)
Purple Sage (W1)
Ransome's Dock (SW11)
Sarastro (WC2)
Sri Siam (W1)
The Stepping Stone (SW8)
The Terrace (W8)
Tom's (W10)
Veeraswamy (W1)
Wagamama (chain)
ZeNW3 (NW3)

DIRECTORY

The Abingdon W8   £17*   A★
54 Abingdon Rd   0171-937 3339   5–2A
It may be only a couple of minutes' walk from the High Street, but this Kensington spot is rather hidden away, in a pleasant residential area, and doesn't attract a great deal of passing trade. More power to the budget diner who seeks out the bargain 2-course lunch, then – for £9.95 (Mon-Fri) you can choose the likes of butternut squash soup, followed by pan-fried fillet of salmon, washed down by house wine at £9.75 a bottle. The 3-course Sunday lunch for £13.50 is also well worth considering. / 11 pm.

Adams Café W12   £17   ★
77 Askew Rd   0181-743 0572   7–1B
Don't be put off by the fact that this long-established Shepherd's Bush spot is a greasy spoon during the day – at night, it becomes a Tunisian/Moroccan bistro of some repute. You know how much you're going to spend, as the menus are prix-fixe only, ranging from the 1-course 'menu rapide' (£9.95) to the 3-course 'menu gastronomique' (£14.95), all including appetisers and mint tea or coffee. Your meal might be brik au thom (tuna filo parcels) followed by couscous with Merguez sausages. BYO (£1.50 per person). / 11 pm; D only.

Afghan Kitchen N1   £10   ★
35 Islington Gn   0171-359 8019   8–3D
For a filling, unusual and extremely affordable pit stop, it is tough to beat this tiny café overlooking Islington Green (though there is little in the way of creature comfort, and service is not the greatest). The ten main dishes on offer (four meat and six veg) are all priced around the £4.50 mark, and served in portions to satisfy the hungriest punter. Rice and a large chunk of bread are £1.50 each, and house wine costs £7.95 a bottle. / 11.30 pm; closed Mon & Sun; no credit cards.

Alba EC1   £17*   -
107 Whitecross St   0171-588 1798   9–1B
Piedmontese cooking is the speciality at this starkly furnished regional Italian near the Barbican. A la carte, it can be quite pricey (unless you stick to the cheaper pastas), but for those on a budget there is a 2-course set menu (£12.90), from which you might choose, say, artichoke, spinach and walnut salad followed by lamb stew. House wine is £10.50 a bottle. / 11 pm; closed Sat & Sun.

Alfred WC2 £19* ★
245 Shaftesbury Ave   0171-240 2566   4–1C
For a taste of what can only be described as true British food, head to this sparsely decorated café-restaurant, north of Covent Garden, for the set 2-course lunch – a steal at £12.95 (and half the cost of a meal à la carte). You might start with whisky-cured smoked salmon followed, perhaps, by crispy pork belly with pickled cabbage, or you could skip the starter and finish up with rice pudding and stewed dates. House wine is £11.75 a bottle. / 11.30 pm; closed Sun.

Ali Baba NW1 £13 ★
32 Ivor Pl   0171-723 5805   8–4A
A quarter of a century on, this pocket-sized Egyptian outfit behind Marylebone Station still attracts a mix of locals and cognoscenti of Middle Eastern cuisine. There is a take-away counter at the front, or you can sit in the rather dimly lit restaurant at the back, sampling good simple dishes such as vine leaves (£4), houmous (£3) or a selection of kebabs and rice (£6). Remember to BYO. / 11.30 pm; no credit cards.

Alma SW18 £15 -
499 Old York Rd   0181-870 2537   10–2B
This large, characterful Wandsworth pub – which is particularly popular with rugby-playing locals – offers the bargain-seeker plenty of scope. Eat in the bar, or head to the rear dining room for a meal which might combine the exotic – say, roast garlic and chicken laksa (£3.95) – with a homely choice such as bangers and mash (£6.50). Drink bitter at £2 a pint, or house wine at £8 a bottle. / 10.30 pm; closed Sun D.

Alounak £14 ★★
10 Russell Gdns, W14   0171-603 1130   7–1D
If you're looking for some real meat cooking at modest cost, you won't do better than this welcoming Olympia Iranian, whose BYO policy helps keep costs low. Lamb is the speciality (though there are also chicken options), with most main dishes somewhere around the £6 mark. Kick off with a selection of meze – £8 for two. There is also a branch in Bayswater (44 Westbourne Grove, W2 tel 0171-229 0416).
/ Midnight; no Amex.

Alphabet W1 £18 𝔸
61-63 Beak St   0171-439 2190   3–2D
This funky Soho hang-out is more of a bar than a restaurant. That said, if you are happy to bide your time for your food – speedy service is not the priority – the eclectic Mediterranean/Thai menu is worth sampling. You might combine stuffed mushrooms and Pecorino (£4) with a Penang chicken curry (£9), washed down with house wine at £10.90 a bottle. / 10.30 pm; closed Sat L & Sun; no Amex; no booking.

Anarkali W6 £18 ★
303-305 King St   0181-748 1760   7–2B
Even regulars would be hard-pushed to spot what changed in the recent refurbishment of this Hammersmith Indian, which – behind its sinister black-tinted windows – has delivered above average curries for over a quarter of a century now. From a menu laden with 'specials', starters are all under £4 (say, kathe – lamb – kebab), and mains are all within the £5-£9 range (for instance jhinya – king prawn – jalpuri). House wine is £8.95, and a pint of Kingfisher is £3.20.
/ Midnight.

Andrew Edmunds W1 £18 A★
46 Lexington St   0171-437 5708   3–2D
This quirky and extremely atmospheric townhouse-bistro is a great favourite, and not just amongst those who are counting their pennies – make sure you book. The modern British cooking is simple but quite interesting – a typical meal might start with feta and bean tabbouleh (£4.25), followed by meatloaf, mash and mushroom sauce (£8). House wine costs £9 a bottle, though if you are willing to splash out a little more, the list affords good drinking. / 10.45 pm.

Anglesea Arms W6 £16 A★
35 Wingate Rd   0181-749 1291   7–1B
This Brackenbury Village gastropub is one of the best examples of the breed – it's a stylish, cosy place serving up notably good modern British cooking at a very fair price. You might start with deep-fried courgette flowers stuffed with goat's cheese (£4.50), followed by char-grilled lamb and chips (£9.50). Wash it down with house wine at £8.95 a bottle, or a pint of Pedigree bitter (£2.40). / 10.30 pm; no Amex; no booking.

Anglo Asian Tandoori N16 £14 A★
60-62 Stoke Newington Ch St   0171-254 9298   1–1C
This low-lit Stoke Newington Indian has more than usual charm, and offers all the traditional dishes at reasonable prices. A meat thali (set meal), for example, is £8.20, with house wine at £7.95 a bottle. On Sundays, the all-you-can-eat buffet lunch (£5.95) is particularly good value. / 11.45 pm, Fri & Sat 12.30 am; no Switch.

Anonimato W10 £18* ★
12 All Saints Rd   0171-243 2808   6–1B
Brightly coloured walls hung with eye-catching pictures provide a suitably artful backdrop for the imaginative, globally-inspired cooking at this stylish North Kensington spot. To keep within our budget, you would have to stick to the cheaper end of the menu, starting with, say, Caesar salad (£5), followed by beetroot risotto (£9.50). Weekend brunch menus also offer budget possibilities. The house wine is £11 a bottle. / 11 pm; D only except Sun, L only.

Antipasto & Pasta SW11 £17 ★★
511 Battersea Park Rd   0171-223 9765   10–1C
Even the standard menu – with a good range of pasta dishes costing around £4-£7 – at this convivial Battersea Italian offers fair value. On Mon, Thu and Sun nights, however, it's a steal, thanks to an all-food-half-price policy. As the name suggests, antipasti are an additional house speciality – at full prices, baked aubergine with parmesan would cost £5. The house wine is £9.50 a bottle. / 11.30 pm; no Amex.

The Apprentice SE1 £18* ★★
31 Shad Thames   0171-234 0254   9–4D
If it's value in the cooking department you're after, look no further than this South Bank school, where the masterchefs of the future learn their trade. The ambience and service are nothing to write home about, but the value of the 3-course set lunch menu (£12.50) is ample compensation – you might have chicken liver parfait, followed by breast of duck and apple tart, washed down with house wine at £9.95 a bottle. A la carte, you would be unlikely to escape within our price-limit. / 8.30 pm; closed Sat & Sun; no smoking area.

Aquarium E1 £20* 𝔸
Ivory Hs, St Katharine-by-the-Tower   0171-480 6116   1–2D
Situated in the heart of St Katharine's Dock, this stark modern British restaurant is an ideal retreat on a summer's day – go early to grab the outside tables. The 2-course set menu (£13.50, always available) offers such delights as pork and truffle salad, followed by roast salmon and polenta – the à la carte is sadly beyond our budget, especially with house wine at City prices (£12 a bottle). / 11 pm; closed Sun, Mon D.

Arancia £17 ★
52 Southwark Park Road, SE16   0171-394 1751   1–3D
The catch is that you have to venture into Bermondsey, but this notable Italian – occupying a cosy corner spot opposite Southwark Park – rewards your efforts with agreeable service and quality cooking. Although the place is entirely containable within our budget à la carte, the best deal is the 3-course dinner (£7.50, the same price as the house wine) – you might choose a starter of linguine with chilli and crab, followed by Sicilian sweet and sour vegetable stew, then rich chocolate semi-freddo to finish. The owners also run the café within the Battersea Arts Centre (Lavender Hill, SW11 tel 0171-223 6557) which is less ambitious, serving Mediterranean tapas.
/ 11 pm; no Amex.

Arkansas Café E1 £16 ★
Unit 12, Old Spitalfield Market   0171-377 6999   9–1D
Amid the hustle and bustle (especially on Sundays) of Spitalfields Market, chef-patron "Bubba" presides over his grill, and serves up basic, but tasty and filling fare to shoppers and stockbrokers alike. The BBQ platter – including ribs, sausages, chicken and all the trimmings – will set you back £9.50. Puddings, if you're still game, are all around the £2 mark, and the extensive American beer list includes bottled Anchor Steam at £2.30. A bottle of the house wine costs £8.75. / L only; closed Sat; no Amex.

Ask! Pizza £15 -
160-162 Victoria St, SW1   0171-630 8228   2–4B
121-125 Park St, W1   0171-495 7760   2–2A
48 Grafton Way, W1   0171-388 8108   2–1B
345 Fulham Palace Rd, SW6   0171-371 0392   10–1B
1 Gloucester Arcade, SW7   0171-835 0840   5–2B
145 Notting Hill Gt, W11   0171-792 9942   6–2B
Whiteleys, 151 Queensway, W2   0171-792 1977   6–1C
219-221 Chiswick High Rd, W4   0181-742 1323   7–2A
222 Kensington High Street, W8   0171-937 5540   5–1A
Bus' Design Ctr, Upper St, N1   0171-226 8728   8–3D
216 Haverstock Hill, NW3   0171-433 3896   8–2A
103 St John Street, EC1   0171-253 0323   9–1A
This recently established but ever-expanding chain, with its modishly cool interiors, seems to be the only one ever likely to challenge the mighty PizzaExpress. Portions are large, and you might choose to start with antipasti (from £1.25), followed by pasta or pizza (both around £6). The house wine is £8.95 a bottle. / 11.30 pm.

Aurora W1 £19   A★
49 Lexington St   0171-494 0514   3–2D
Low evening lighting at this intimate Soho eatery makes it a popular romantic destination, and, for the daytime, there's a sweet courtyard at the back. The cooking is also part of the attraction – start, perhaps, with a salad of chicory and caramelised peaches (£5.50) followed by pan-fried salmon with plantain and coconut rice (£9.50). BYO – corkage is £2.50 a bottle (though the policy is currently under review). Cakes, coffee and Saturday brunch are further attractions.
/ 10.30 pm; closed Sun; no Amex.

Babur Brasserie SE23 £18   ★★
119 Brockley Rise, Forest Hill   0181-291 2400   1–4D
Cooking far from that of your generic curry house has created a deserved reputation for this Forest Hill Indian. The only set menu here is vegetarian (£11.75), and regional specialities (which change periodically) are the order of the day. A typical meal might be spiced crab meat (£4.95) followed by monkfish curry with coriander (£8.95), and if you're in any doubt as to your menu choice, you will find the staff delighted to help. The house wine is £7.95 a bottle. / 11.15 pm; Fri L; no smoking area.

Balans £17   A
60 Old Compton St, W1   0171-437 5212   4–3A
239 Old Brompton Rd, SW5   0171-244 8838   5–3A
Though they've got quite a big gay following, these Soho and Earl's Court bistros attract all sorts at all hours with their bright décor and breezy welcome. The food has no great pretensions, but dishes such as quesadillas (£4.50) and chicken with green mango salsa (£8.50) are all perfectly well done, and breakfasts (full works, £5.50) are also a strong point. The house wine is £9.75 a bottle. / W1 Mon-Sat 3 am, Sun 1 am – SW5 1 am; W1 no booking – SW5 Sat & Sun no booking.

Bangkok SW7 £19   ★
9 Bute St   0171-584 8529   5–2B
No one ever goes to this '60s South Kensington Thai – which claims to be the oldest in the UK – in search of excitement. Utter consistency, however, keeps a steady flow of locals and visitors coming back for traditional starters such as beef satay (£5.20) and main courses such as beef curry with crispy Thai basil (£6.80) and rice (£2). The house wine – expensive in the context of the minimal comfort level – is £9.90 a bottle.
/ 11 pm; closed Sun; no Amex.

Bank WC2 £20* 𝔸★
1 Kingsway   0171-379 9797   2–2D
If you want to check out one of the mega-brasseries which have been the talk of the town in recent years, this stylish Aldwych spot rates among the best. There's nearly always a budget option available – the all-day breakfast or brunch will set you back around a tenner, and at lunch or pre-theatre (5.30pm-7.30pm) there's a 2-course set menu – from which you might choose fish sausages with warm lentil salad, followed by pear and ginger sponge – for £13.90. The house wine is a not immodest £12.50 a bottle. / 11 pm; no Switch.

Bar Gansa NW1 £13 𝔸★
2 Inverness St   0171-267 8909   8–3B
This buzzing Camden Town tapas bar serves up good and inexpensive snacks, such as meatballs (£3.25), tortillas (£3) and calamari (£3.60) to the trendy twentysomethings of north London. More substantial dishes are available at around £6-£7, and house wine is £8.95 a bottle. / Midnight; no Amex.

Bar Italia W1 £6 𝔸
22 Frith St   0171-437 4520   4–2A
A long-established cult venue for Soho trendies, this very Italian coffee bar, open almost all hours, is well known as the quintessential post-clubbing hang-out. The food, of course, is not the main attraction, but runs to the likes of sandwiches (£3.50) and light pasta dishes (£3). No alcohol – wash down your snack with an espresso or cappuccino (£1.40) or fresh juices (from £2.20). / 4 am, Fri & Sat 24 hours; no credit cards; no booking.

Bar Japan SW5 £15 -
251 Old Brompton Rd   0171-370 2323   5–3A
Fun, if basic, Earl's Court café which makes a good bet for a quick and interesting bite. Service is friendly, and the sushi is better than at many budget places – a plate of six salmon and tuna sushi pieces costs £4.50. House wine is £9.50 a bottle, or drink green tea for £1. / 10.45 pm.

Barcelona Tapas £14 ★
1a Bell Ln, E1   0171-247 7014   9–2D
1 Beaufort Hs, St Botolph St, EC3   0171-377 5222   9–2D
They couldn't be more superficially different – one at the base of a shiny, new skyscraper, the other in a basement off a chaotic street market – but these City tapas bars both offer similarly authentic tapas (from under a long glass counter), many costing under £3. You could make a meal of these, or two people (minimum) could opt for paella (£10.95 each). The house wine is £9.50 a bottle. / 10 pm; closed Sat & Sun D.

Battersea Rickshaw SW11 £15 -
15-16 Battersea Sq   0171-924 2450   5–4C
It's never going to set the world on fire, but this smarter-than-average Battersea Indian offers all the usual curries (generally around £6), at a standard a cut above the norm, in comfortable (if rather dull) surroundings. The house wine is £9.50 a bottle. / 11.30 pm; D only.

Bedlington Café W4 £15 ★
24 Fauconberg Rd   0181-994 1965   7–2A
This informal – scruffy, some might say – Chiswick greasy spoon was one of the first to make a name for itself by offering authentic, fiercely spiced and reasonably priced Thai dinners. Frankly, it's not what it used to be, but still offers good-value cooking – with most main courses around £7.50 – and costs are held down by bringing your own wine (60p corkage). There's an off-licence practically next door. / 10 pm; no credit cards; no smoking area.

Beirut Express W2 £18 ★
112-114 Edgware Rd   0171-724 2700   6–1D
Lebanon comes to London and at this extremely authentic corner pit stop (part of the highly successful Maroush group) where lovers of Middle Eastern cooking can enjoy excellent mezze in smart café surroundings. Prices are affordable, if not bargain basement (tabbouleh and houmous are both £3.90), and the best budget policy is to go for the meze (£3.50-£5), rather than the good but not inexpensive main dishes (baby chicken stuffed with rice, minced meat and pine kernels, £12). No alcohol is served, but they do some delicious juices, for example mango (£1.60). / 1.45 am; no credit cards.

Ben's Thai W9 £15 A★
93 Warrington Cr   0171-266 3134   8–4A
This first-floor dining-room of a palatial Victorian pub (The Warrington Hotel) in Maida Vale provides the rather unlikely setting for one of the best-value (and most characterful) Thai eating places in town – it's best to book. Starters, such as spring rolls, are £2.95, and a dish such as sweet and sour fish is £7. The house wine is £8 a bottle. Tipping is discouraged.
/ 10 pm; D only; no Amex & no Switch.

Benihana £18* A★
37-43 Sackville St, W1   494 2525   3–3D
77 King's Rd, SW3   376 7799   5–3D
100 Avenue Rd, NW3   586 9508   8–2A
Japanese cooking, American-style, is the proposition at this glitzy international chain. It's very pricey à la carte, but the set lunch specials offer surprisingly good value. They change throughout the year, but generally combine some form of protein, say chicken teriyaki, with vegetables, rice and green tea, and cost £10-£12. The house wine is £11.50 a bottle. / 10 pm, Fri & Sat Midnight.

Bersagliera SW3 £16 -
372 King's Rd   0171-352 5993   5–3B
It's worth braving the din at this basic World's End trattoria for some of the best-value food in that part of town. You might have deep-fried calamari with courgettes (£5.90), and then, to stay within budget, one of the wide range of pizza or home-made pasta dishes (all £5-£7). The house wine wine is £9.60 a bottle. / Midnight; closed Sun; no Amex.

Beyoglu SW11 £15 ★★
50 Battersea Pk Rd   0171-627 2052   10–1C
Really good Turkish cooking at bargain prices has won quite a following for this down-to-earth Battersea spot. You might combine the likes of aubergine salad (£2.60), with mixed kebabs and rice (£8), or share the £21 set meal for two, which includes meze and main dishes. The house wine is £7.50 a bottle. / 11 pm; closed Sun; no Amex & no Switch.

Blah! Blah! Blah! W12 £17 ★
78 Goldhawk Rd   0181-746 1337   7–1C
An unusually lively and stylish place – for a veggie – this Shepherd's Bush bistro maintains quite a chic following. The cooking's quite good, too – your main course might be crespollini with ricotta, pepperonata and Gorgonzola sauce (£7.95), and you could finish with a banana and choux pastry gâteau (£4.95). The BYO policy with modestly priced corkage (95p a bottle) contributes to the jolly atmosphere. / 11 pm; closed Sun; no credit cards.

Blue Jade SW1 £16 -
44 Hugh St   0171-828 0321   2–4B
This comfortable Thai restaurant comes as something of a surprise in its dark Pimlico back street setting. Most starters, such as 'money bags' (pork, prawn and crab with Thai herbs, deep-fried in pastry) are around the £4 mark. At £8.50 – a pound less than a bottle of the house vino – prawn red curry is one of the more expensive main course options. / 11 pm; closed Sat L & Sun.

Bluebird SW3 £20* A★
350 Kings Rd   0171-559 1000   5–3C
The set lunch and pre-theatre menus (until 7pm) at this airy and impressive Chelsea edifice (with de luxe foodmarket below) allow you to check out one of the flagships of London's best-known restaurant groupings – Conran Restaurants. For £12.75 (the same price as a bottle of the house wine), your 2-course selection might be pumpkin soup followed by chicken Kiev. / 11.30 pm.

Blues W1 £18* A★
42 Dean St   0171-494 1966   4–2A
On a Saturday night until 7.30pm (also Mon and Tue, 6pm-8pm), small parties (less than four) can enjoy a 3-course meal at this trendy Soho joint for a mere £10 a head. The modern British fare might include celeriac soup followed by char-grilled pork, with strawberry mousse to finish. At other times, choose carefully to stay within budget (easier if you're a veggie), or go for the 2-course lunch, also at £10. House wine is £10.95 a bottle. / 11.30 pm, Thu-Sat midnight; closed Sat L.

Blythe Road Restaurant W14 £19* A★
71 Blythe Rd   0171-371 3635   7–1C
This agreeable Brook Green neighbourhood restaurant provides a variety if set lunch options – 1-course (£7.50), 2-course (£10), and 3-course (£12.50) menus. If you decide to go for the Full Monty, you might have broccoli & Stilton soup, followed by wild boar sausages, with lemon posset for dessert. A bottle of the house wine is £9.50. / 10.30 pm; closed Sat L & Sun.

Boiled Egg & Soldiers SW11 £11 -
63 Northcote Rd   0171-223 4894   10–2C
An interesting mix of customers – from nannies with infants in pushchairs, to hungover twentysomethings in search of a restorative fry-up – gather at this crowded Common-sider, attracted by the all-day breakfast-and-comfort-food formula. Tuck into a full English breakfast (£4.50), main courses such as spicy lamb pie (£3.25) or a cake (banana and walnut slice, £1.35). Wash it all down with a pot of strong tea (95p), or a bottle of house wine (£7.50). Marmite soldiers (50p) may help to keep the children quiet. / 6 pm; no credit cards; no booking.

Boudin Blanc W1 £14* A★
5 Trebeck St   0171-499 3292   3–4B
This comfortable, if tightly packed, Gallic bistro is characterfully located in Mayfair's Shepherd Market – it's one of our top choices in the centre of town. Best value of all is the 2-course set menu (£6.85) available until 7pm, from which you might choose Vichyssoise, then Toulouse sausage and frites. Thereafter, to stay within our budget, you would have to opt for the 3-course set menu (£10.95), which is always available. House wine is £9.95 a bottle. / 11 pm.

Brady's SW18 £12 -
513 Old York Rd   0181-877 9599   10–2B
Mr Brady's well-established fish and chip bistro in Wandsworth offers a bistro-style setting to enjoy well cooked examples of our (under-rated) Great National Dish. Cod 'n' chips will set you back £5, and, to finish, there's a good treacle tart (£1.95). The house wine is £9.50 a bottle.
/ 10.30 pm; closed Sun; no credit cards; no booking.

Brahms SW1 £10 -
147 Lupus St   0171-834 9075   5–3D
There aren't that many places where you can find a real 3-course meal comfortably within our price bracket, but the £5 set lunch (and pre-7.15pm) menu at this Pimlico bistro (previously called Little Bay and still part of the same group) certainly fits the bill. Even á la carte, you're hardly likely to break the bank. Starters, perhaps baked goat's cheese in filo pastry (£2.20), offer real value, and even a top-end main course, like lamb in Madeira sauce, is a mere £5.45. The house wine is £7.95 a bottle. / 11.45 pm; no credit cards.

Brass. du Marché aux Puces W10 £15* A★
349 Portobello Rd   0181-968 5828   6–1A
This fashionable North Kensington bistro may sound thoroughly French, but its menu is in fact quite eclectic. Best weekday value – and the only real choice if you want to stay comfortably within our budget – is the 2-course set lunch menu served all-day for £9.50, including coffee. Grilled Scottish salmon with chips is a staple, and puddings are the likes of crème brûlée. At weekends, there's brunch (£8.50) and also a 3-course Sunday lunch (£12.50). House wine is £9.95 a bottle. / 11.30 pm; closed Sun D; no Amex.

Brick Lane Beigel Bake E1 £ 3 ★
159 Brick Ln   0171-729 0616   1–2D
You might find a queue at any time of the day (or night) at this all-hours East End institution, which is probably as well known as the street in which it is situated. The attraction? – delicious filled beigels, such as smoked salmon and cream cheese (95p) or tuna (65p), washed down with a large cup of tea (35p) or coffee (40p). / 24 hr; no credit cards.

Brilliant UB2 £14 ★★
72-76 Western Rd   0181-574 1928   1–3A
A point of pilgrimmage for curry-lovers – this famous suburban curry house occupies a large site, ten minutes walk from Southall BR. Prices are keen and quality high – you might share a tandoori paneer tikka to start (£7.50 for two), with a Pallak chicken and spinach curry to follow (£6). A bottle of house wine is £7.50, or drink Cobra at £3.20 a bottle. / 11 pm; closed Mon, Sat L & Sun L.

Bu San N7 £14 ★
43 Holloway Rd   0171-607 8264   8–2D
This lesser-known Korean – just round the corner from Highbury and Islington tube – may have an inauspicous-looking facade, but serves up surprisingly good food. A la carte, you could try deep-fried aubergine (£2.60) followed by sizzling marinated ribs (£6.90). If you are in the area for lunch there's a selection of one-course lunch menus for £4-£7, including rice and tea. House wine is £8.95 a bottle. / 11.30 pm; closed Sat L & Sun L; no Amex.

Buchan's SW11 £14* 𝔸
62-64 Battersea Br Rd   0171-228 0888   5–4C
This bustling wine bar/bistro, just over Battersea Bridge, provides modern Scottish cooking of good quality, and offers plenty of enticements to the budget-conscious diner. The 2-course set lunch will set you back about £8.50 (£11.50, Sun), and there is also a 2-course dinner on Mon & Sun evenings for £8.95 – you might choose lobster bisque followed by marinated duck. The house wine is £9.95 a bottle. / 10.45 pm.

Buona Sera SW11 £17 𝔸
22 Northcote Rd   0171-228 9925   10–2C
This ever-buzzing Battersea Italian is a long-running local success story thanks to the reliable quality of its long, fairly traditional menu – there are all the usual pizza and pasta dishes (around £6), or you could opt for deep-fried courgettes and squid (£4.80) followed by steak in a red wine sauce (£8.50). House wine is a modest £7.30 a bottle. A branch opened in Covent Garden as we went to press (43 Drury Lane WC2, tel 0171-836 8296). / Midnight; no Amex.

The Butlers Wharf Chop-house SE1 £15* ★
36e Shad Thames   0171-403 3403   9–4D
The proximity of all those City moneybags, just over the river, keep restaurant prices high at this modern English chop-house. The bar menu, though, offers two courses for £7.75 – perhaps chicken and apricot stew followed by walnut and honey tart – or three for £9.50. At weekends a 2-course brunch menu is offered for £13.95. The house wine is £11.95 a bottle. / *11 pm; closed Sat L & Sun D.*

Café 206 W11   **£17**   ★
206 Westbourne Grove   0171-221 1535   6–1B
This friendly and busy all-day Italian café and restaurant is a popular Notting Hill haunt. You can pop in for a sandwich and a cup of coffee, or, for something more substantial, try the home-made minestrone (£3.95), with grilled chicken and polenta (£7.50) to follow. The house wine is £9.95 a bottle.
/ *6.30 pm; L only; closed Sat D & Sun D; no Amex.*

Café Bohème W1   **£20***   𝔸
17 Old Compton St   0171-734 0623   4–2A
It's certainly not a foodie haunt, but this (suitably enough) Bohemian Soho lynch-pin – combining bar, café and restaurant – has other attractions, especially for younger souls looking for somewhere to go at any time of the day or night (24-hrs Thu-Sat; entry charge after 10pm of up to £4). You will have to choose quite carefully to stay within our price limit – you might have seafood and saffron soup (£3.95), followed by chicken with wild rice (£8.95), washed down with house wine at £8.90 a bottle. / *2.45 am, Thu-Sat open 24 hours, Sun 11.30 pm.*

Café Coq WC2   **£14**   ★
154-156 Shaftesbury Ave   0171-836 8635   4–2B
It's quite difficult to find plain protein at modest cost in the West End, so this stark new rôtisserie near Cambridge Circus is worth remembering. Half a spit-roasted chicken with frites will set you back £9 – the same price as a bottle of the house wine. A starter of grilled halloumi with salad costs £3. / *11 pm; closed Sun L; bookings only for 10+.*

Café de la Place SW11   **£14**   ★
11-12 Battersea Sq   0171-978 5374   5–4C
This all-day Battersea bistro is the sort of place where you can have an English breakfast, drop in throughout the day for a sandwich and a coffee, or eat 'properly' at meal times. A la carte prices are modest, but there is also a simple 2-course lunch – perhaps pâté followed by beef casserole (£7.50) – and in the evening, there is a slightly more ambitious 3-course menu for £11.95. The house wine is £8.95 a bottle. / *11 pm; closed Sun D; no Amex.*

Café du Jardin WC2 £17* 🅐★
28 Wellington St   0171-836 8769   4–3D
If you are looking to eat around Covent Garden, this modern British corner-restaurant is well worth knowing about for its set menus (à la carte, you could easily blow our budget twice over). Available at lunchtime and pre-theatre (5.30pm-7.30pm), there are both 2-course (£9.95, including coffee) and 3-course (£13.50) options – you might have tomato penne, salmon with herb mash and white chocolate mousse to finish. House wine starts at £9.50 a bottle.
/ *Midnight.*

Café Emm W1 £16 -
17 Frith St   0171-437 0723   4–2A
This cosy, but loud central Soho bistro offers reliable and tasty modern British fare at reasonable prices, and is, quite rightly, always busy. Starters are £4.50, and mains – which might be Cajun chicken, vegetable crêpes or falafel – all cost £6.50. House wine is quite pricey at £9.80 a bottle. / 10.30 pm, Fri & Sat 12.30 am; closed Sat L & Sun L; no Amex; book L only.

Café Fish W1 £15* -
36-40 Rupert Street   0171-287 8989   3–0
Billing itself as a 'canteen' by day, and a 'restaurant' by night, this Theatreland fish specialist occupies spacious new premises just off Shaftesbury Avenue. It's generally a little out of our price range, unless you go for the 2-course set meal (£10, available from lunch until the 7pm metamorphosis) – from which you might choose prawn soup followed by seafood pie. House wine is £8 a bottle. / 11.30 pm; no smoking area.

Café Grove W11 £12 🅐
253a Portobello Rd   0171-243 1094   6–1A
Chilling out on the large balcony overlooking the street market is a top attraction at this simple, first-floor Portobello café. A full carnivore's breakfast costs £6.75, sandwiches start at £2, and more filling meals, such as lasagne (£5.50), are also available. A bottle of the house wine is £6.95. / winter 5 pm, summer 10.30 pm; winter L only – summer, closed Sat D & Sun D; no credit cards; need 10+ to book.

Café Indiya E1 £17 ★
30 Alie St   0171-481 8288   9–3D
It's certainly bright and modern, and this east-City Indian offers good cooking at reasonable prices. Fish tikka, to start, would be £3.95, for example, curries are around the £6 mark, and the house wine is £7.95 a bottle. There's something about the atmosphere, though, that makes this a place to 'eat and go', rather than to spend an evening. / 11 pm; closed Sat & Sun.

Café Japan NW11 £17 ★
626 Finchley Rd   0181-455 6854   1–1B
A welcoming grunt often greets diners at this cheerful Japanese, near Golder's Green Station. The cooking is of good quality and the best value options are the set menus – for £12 you get chicken yakitori (skewers), miso, salad and rice. Alternatively, £10.50 for 13 pieces of sushi is quite an attractive deal. House wine is £8.50 a bottle, and Japanese beers cost around £4. / 10.30 pm; D only; no Amex.

Café Latino W1 £17 A
25 Frith St   0171-287 5676   4–2A
The welcome is genuinely friendly at this vibrant, modern Soho establishment. Its Latin American tapas menu lists dishes such as roast garlic and goat's cheese (£2.50) and fish cooked with lime and coconut (£3.95) alongside more familiar tapas dishes, which are generally under a fiver. House wine will cost you £8.95 a bottle. A sibling has recently opened in Islington, at 144 Upper Street, N1 (tel 0171-704 6868).
/ 11 pm, Thu-Sat 1 am.

Café Montpeliano SW3 £18 A
144 Brompton Rd   0171-225 2926   5–1C
In the pricey environs of Harrods, this smart Italian café-bistro is especially worth knowing about. Bruschetta (£4.50), pastas (£5.95) and salad platters (£7.50) are the sorts of dishes which prepare ladies who lunch for their afternoon assault on the stores. The house wine is £9.50 a bottle. / 11 pm; closed Sun D; no Switch.

Café Mozart N6 £12 -
17 Swains Lane   0181-348 1384   8–1B
London would be a better place if every part of town had a hang-out like this Hampstead Heath-fringe coffee-house-cum-bistro. Apart from the thoroughly English breakfasts (£3.95), there's a Mitteleuropean twist to most of the dishes, so the special of the day might be a spicy vegetable goulash (£5.95), for example, and there are salads and fancy sandwiches (£4-£6) too. The house wine is £8.50 a bottle. / 10 pm; no Amex; no smoking; no booking at L.

Café O SW3 £16* ★
163 Draycott Ave   0171-584 5950   5–2C
A more generally Mediterranean drift has recently been given to this formerly exclusively Greek establishment near Brompton Cross. Presumably it's all a ploy to attract the ladies who lunch, as surprisingly low prices (for the area) never really attracted quite the following the place deserved. As house wines starting at £10.90 a bottle suggest, you will have to choose carefully to stay within budget – perhaps vegetable risotto with saffron (£4.50) followed by mushrooms stuffed with prawns and dill (£7.20). / 11 pm; closed Sun.

Café Portugal SW8 £16 ★
5a & 6a Victoria Hs, S Lambeth Rd   0171-587 1962   10–1D
For a Portuguese dinner without ceremony or pretence, it's worth seeking out this family-run Vauxhall spot (which, by day, is a café). Prices are not demanding – cream of seafood soup, for example, costs £2.50, and a smoked meat and bean stew is £7.50. The house wine is £8.50 a bottle. / 11 pm; no Amex.

Café Sofra £9 -
10 Shepherd Mkt, W1   0171-495 3434   3–4B
33 Old Compton St, W1   0171-494 0222   4–2A
63 Wigmore St, W1   0171-486 7788   3–1A
145 High Holborn, WC1   0171-430 0430   2–1D
15 Catherine St, WC2   0171-240 9991   4–3D
5 Garrick St, WC2   0171-240 6688   4–3C
101 Fleet St, EC4   0171-583 6669   9–2A
This chain of bright, colourful cafes continues to grow in popularity, thanks to the quality of their light, basic Lebanese/Turkish fare. These are not what you could call comfortable places, and service can be distracted, but at these prices, who'd complain? Mezes, hot falafel sandwiches and tasty casseroles, all between £2 and £5, can be followed up with gooey baklava (50p a piece). BYO (no charge). Take-away available. / Midnight, Old Compton St 2 am, EC4 9 pm; no credit cards; no smoking area; no booking.

Café Spice Namaste E1 £20* ★
16 Prescot St   0171-488 9242   1–2D
This large, brightly furnished east-City spot offers some of the most interesting Indian cooking in town and, unusually, the menu is always evolving, thanks to chef Cyrus Todiwala's innovative use of seasonal ingredients. With house wine at £11 a bottle, you'll have to eat quite modestly to stay within our budget, but with some starters around £3 and the less exotic curry dishes around £9, it is just possible. There is a Battersea offshoot (not listed), in which we can see little attraction. / 10.30 pm; closed Sat L & Sun.

Calabash WC2 £14 ★
38 King St   0171-836 1976   4–3C
*Desperate to escape the ersatz trendiness of Covent Garden?
– dive into the musty basement of the very '60s Africa
Centre. Here you'll find soft African music – except when
they're drumming, of course – and authentic African cuisine.
If you've never had gizzard (chicken stomach with onions and
green peppers, £2.95), now's your chance, or you could try
the Calabash Special (£6.25) – either fish or chicken with
sweet potatoes and plantain. African wines are available from
£7.50 a bottle.* / 10.30 pm; closed Sat L & Sun; no Switch.

Cantaloupe EC2 £10*   A★
35-42 Charlotte Rd   0171-613 4411   9–1D
*Long (well, a couple of years) at the vanguard of the
trendification of Clerkenwell, this buzzing bar-restaurant
maintains its grip on the affections of local Bohemians. If you
eat in the restaurant at the back (recently extended), you
would spend a little outside our price-limit, but there are very
tasty bar snacks/tapas to be had – perhaps grilled mussels
with garlic salsa (£4) or fried chorizo and chickpeas (£3).
The bar offers a choice of just about every alcoholic beverage
known to man, including house wine at £8.90 a bottle.*
/ Midnight; closed Sat L; no Amex; no smoking area.

Cantina Italia N1 £17   ★
19 Canonbury Lane   0171-226 9791   8–2D
*Many people who follow restaurants (including us) feel that
the future lies in restaurants which set out to deliver satisfying
grub in unpretentious surroundings. That bodes well for this
Islington Italian, which serves up reliable pizzas and pastas
(all around £7) and so on in a rather bare setting – avoid the
basement. The house wine is £9.80 a bottle.* / 11.30 pm;
no Amex.

Cantinetto Venegazzú SW11 £17   ★
31–32 Battersea Sq   0171-978 5395   5–4C
*It may offer unusually interesting Venetian food, but rather
poky surroundings help ensure that prices stay reasonable at
this small Battersea newcomer – it's nicest on sunny days,
when you can sit outside in the square. You might start with
gratinated oysters (£4.90), followed, for economy, by a pasta
or risotto (around £7), washed down by house wine at £9.90
a bottle. A 2-course weekday lunch is offered at £5.90.*
/ 11.30 pm.

Carnevale EC1 £17 ★
135 Whitecross St   0171-250 3452   9–1B
Proximity to the City means that this very popular, but tiny veggie can charge fairly hefty prices – most starters are a fiver and most main courses around the £8.50 mark. Best value is the lunch and early-evening menu (ideal pre-Barbican) from which, for £9.95, you can have three courses (or two courses and a drink). You might start with black bean enchiladas with tomato salsa, followed by saffron spaghettini with oyster mushrooms and artichokes, with apple bread pudding to finish. The house wine is £9.50 a bottle.
/ 10.30 pm; closed Sun; switch only.

Centuria N1 £18 -
100 St Paul's Rd   0171-704 2435   1–1C
The larger-than-usual rear dining room of this spacious north Islington gastropub is a bit lacking, atmosphere-wise, so it's probably better, space permitting, to grab a spot in the bar at the front. You can get the full menu there too, so you might choose from the likes of rib-eye steak in brandy sauce (£9) or roast cod with chicory (£8.75). The house wine is £9 a bottle.
/ 11 pm; closed weekday L; no Amex.

The Chapel NW1 £17 ★
48 Chapel St   0171-402 9220   6–1D
The blackboard menu changes daily at this lively gastropub – just along the road from Edgware Road tube – whose fans don't mind that it tends to be smoky, cramped and noisy. You might have broccoli, Stilton and almond tart (£5), followed by pan-fried salmon (£9.75), and wash it all down with the house wine (£8.80 a bottle), or a pint of Staropramen (£2.80).
/ 9.50 pm.

Chelsea Kitchen SW3 £8 ★
98 King's Rd   0171-589 1330   5–2D
OK, the food's nothing special, but this diner, located only a hundred yards from Sloane Square, is truly remarkable for offering today pretty much the same formula of 'unpretentious nosh for not very much dosh' which first made it a success over 30 years ago. (Within living memory, everything was priced to the penny.) Set menus – perhaps soup, chicken Kiev and crumble – will set you back about £6 (which is also the price of a bottle of the house vino), or you can dine à la carte for not much more. / 11.30 pm; no credit cards; no smoking area; need 4+ to book.

Chelsea Ram SW10   £16   ★★
32 Burnaby St   0171-351 4008   5–4B
It may not have the most charming Chelsea location (nestling, as it does, near the Lot's Road power station), but it's still well worth seeking out this jolly gastropub – its modern British fare is among the best-value in town. You will have to choose quite carefully to stay within our price limit, but if you had salmon carpaccio (£4.95) followed by chicken, bacon and avocado salad (£7.95), for example, it's perfectly possible. The house wine is £8.95 a bottle, or a pint of Young's is £2. / 10 pm; Sun 9 pm; no Amex; no booking.

Chez Liline N4   £19*   ★★
101 Stroud Green Rd   0171-263 6550   8–1D
Admittedly you have to trek to Finsbury Park to get it, but this rather grim-looking Mauritian fish restaurant really does offer some of the most interesting and best-value cooking to be had in London. Even dining à la carte and from a menu which specialises in tropical fish, you could just about keep within our price limit, but there's certainly no problem if you choose from the 2-course set menu (£12.75, always available) – your choice might be avocado and crab salad followed by red snapper in Creole sauce, washed down by house wine at £10.25 a bottle. / 10.30 pm; closed Sun.

Chiang Mai W1   £20   ★★
48 Frith St   0171-437 7444   4–2A
It's nothing to look at, but this Thai restaurant in the heart of Soho is one of the best in terms of the quality of its cooking (and it offers a particularly wide selection for veggies). The menu (which is slanted towards northern Thailand) includes dishes such as spicy fishcakes (£6.55) and lemon-grass curry (£7.25). House wine, at £10.50 a bottle, is surprisingly expensive. / 11 pm; closed Sun L.

China City WC2   £16   -
25a Lisle St   0171-734 3388   4–3A
Not only its cute little hidden courtyard and smartish surroundings, but also the fresh and flavoursome fare set this place apart from other Chinatown behemoths. From the encyclopeadeic menu you might choose seafood and straw noodle soup (£3.50) and follow it with chicken in ginger and onion sauce (£8.50). House wine is £8 a bottle. / 11.45 pm; no smoking area; Sun, no lunch bookings.

Chiswick Restaurant W4   £16*   ★★
131-133 Chiswick High Rd   0181-994 6887   7–2B
For a local restaurant, this Chiswick spot offers some of the best modern British cooking in town, even if you do have to consume it in surroundings which may strike some as unnecessarily bleak. It's out of our price-range à la carte, but at lunchtime and before 8pm, there's a good-value 2-course menu, including coffee, for £9.50. You might have sweet and sour aubergine salad followed by roast cod with lemon couscous. The house wine is £10.50 a bottle. / 11 pm; closed Sat L & Sun D.

Chuen Cheng Ku W1   £17   -
17 Wardour St   0171-437 1398   4–3A
No Chinatown spot is more 'classic' than this gaudy behemoth. The lunchtime dim sum (served from trolleys, £1.80 a dish) are the top attraction. In the evening, the place is no more than a standby – the cheapest set menu, at £13, includes healthy-size portions of unremarkable fare. House wine is £9.50 a bottle, or a flask of saki is £4.50. / 11.45 pm; no smoking area.

Churchill W8   £9   Ⓐ★
119 Kensington Ch St   0171-792 1246   6–2B
It's best to book if you want to secure a seat in the conservatory-annexe of this popular Kensington Thai gastro-boozer, which is famed for the one-plate dishes, all priced under a fiver. The 20 choices include stir-fried pork with prawns and fresh chilli, or stir-fried beef and peppers with oyster sauce. All dishes come with rice. The house wine is £8.95 a bottle. / 9.30 pm; closed Sun D; no Amex; no lunch bookings.

Chutney Mary SW10   £18*   Ⓐ★
535 King's Rd   0171-351 3113   5–4B
A slightly isolated location – on the Fulham-fringe of Chelsea – does nothing to diminish the popularity of this grand (and recently refurbished) Indian restaurant. It's not really in our price-limit à la carte, but there's a 2-course set lunch for £12.50, which might comprise spicy Goan fishcakes and tandoori Afghani chicken. The house wine is £10.95 a bottle. / 11.30 pm; no smoking area.

Chutneys NW1   £10   ★
124 Drummond St   0171-388 0604   8–4C
This vegetarian restaurant in the Little India near Euston station is best known for its lunchtime buffet (£4.95), also served all day on Sunday. Even à la carte, though, you'd be hard pushed to breach our budget, as most dishes are under a fiver. The house wine is £5.95 a bottle, or £1 more for organic. / 11 pm; no Amex & no Switch; bookings 10+ only on Sun.

Cibo W14 £18* A★★
3 Russell Gdns   0171-371 6271   7–1D
You can tell the cooking at this Italian restaurant is good. Otherwise, there's no way somewhere so expensive – well out of our range, à la carte – could have survived in its obscure location near the railway tracks at Olympia. Given this quality, therefore, the £12.50 2-course set lunch is a true bargain – you might choose wild rocket, tomato & clam salad, followed by roast poussin with garlic and lemon. The house wine is £10.50 a bottle. / 11 pm; closed Sat L & Sun D; smart casual.

Coins W11 £14 A
105-107 Talbot Rd   0171-221 8099   6–1B
Popularity with the trustafarians of Notting Hill means that this airy and artified all-day café now opens for dinner, too (Tue-Fri), though it's still as a cool brunch spot that it's best known. If you're visiting for a more serious meal, you might start off with roast yellow pepper and garlic soup (£3.50), followed by lentil stew with chorizo (£6.50). The house wine is a tenner a bottle. / 10pm; closed Sat-Mon D.

Coopers Arms SW3 £17 A★
87 Flood St   0171-376 3120   5–3C
The popularity of this stylish and convivial Chelsea boozer belies its backstreet location. The menu changes daily, and is surprisingly ambitious – you might have a breakfast salad (with bacon, sausage, white pudding and fried quail's eggs), (£4.75), followed by chicken with Brie and sun-dried tomatoes (£8.25). Wines start at around £9 a bottle, or you could have a pint of Young's bitter for £2. / 10 pm; no bookings Sun .

Corney & Barrow WC2 £16* ★
116 St Martin's Lane   0171-655 9800   4–4B
Unlikely as it may seem, the stylish (if chilling) West End outpost of this upmarket City wine bar chain is one of the better choices for an inexpensive (if not exactly hearty) lunch or pre-theatre dinner – the 2-course menu (£9.95) might offer smoked mackerel salad followed by moules and frites. Wine starts at £10.95 a bottle, or you can blow all this economy nonsense with a trip to the basement champagne bar. / 11.15 pm; closed Sun.

Costa's Fish Restaurant W8 £10 ★
18 Hillgate St   0171-727 4310   6–2B
This long-established chippy, just off Notting Hill Gate, is often eclipsed by its larger and more famous neighbour, Geale's – which is a shame as it's one of the top-value spots in this not inexpensive part of town. Cod, haddock, lemon sole and plaice – all served with chips, salad or mushy peas – are around £5.50. You can wash all this down with house wine at £6.90 a bottle. / 10 pm; closed Mon & Sun; no credit cards.

Costa's Grill W8 £10 A★
12-14 Hillgate St   0171-229 3794   6–2B
Greek dishes are served in generous portions at this modest restaurant just behind Notting Hill Gate, which has that certain charm which goes with having been run by the same family for the past 40 years. Prices are not aggressively contemporary, and dishes include calamari (£2) and taramasalata with pitta bread (£1.50). For a main course, you might sample the souvlakia – lamb on the spit (£5). A bottle of Greek or Cypriot house wine will set you back £6.50.
/ 10.30 pm; closed Sun; no credit cards.

Coyote Café W4 £16 -
2 Fauconberg Road   0181-742 8545   7–2A
There's precious little in the way of quality south west American (or Mexican) food to be had in London, so if you like that sort of thing it's probably worth the trip to this Chiswick cantina for the competent nachos (£5.95), fajitas (£8.95) and the like – at lunchtime, the menu is more about burgers and so on. House wine seems rather pricey at £10.95 a bottle. / 10 pm; no large bookings on Fri & Sat.

The Crescent SW3 £18 A
99 Fulham Rd   0171-225 2244   5–2C
The owners prefer this Brompton Cross spot to be regarded as a wine bar rather than a bistro, and who can argue when you discover it offers a range of over 200 wines (from £9.50 a bottle), including an impressive selection by the glass. For those who are hungry, there is a snack menu offering an eclectic range of food such as spring rolls and calamari (both £3.95), and, for something more substantial, burgers (from £5.95). This is also quite a cool place for breakfast. / 11 pm; no booking.

The Cross Keys SW3 £15* A
1 Lawrence St   0171-349 9111   5–3C
Located just behind Chelsea's Cheyne Walk (houses £5 million and up), this fashionably revamped pub attracts a crowd which is not short of a bob or two. Dining à la carte in the rear conservatory restaurant is a touch outside our budget, but the 2-course Sunday lunch (£10.50) comes within it – you might have a tricolore salad followed by the roast or a seared tuna steak. Otherwise, the best deal is the £7.50, 2-course set lunch (Mon-Sat). The house wine is £10.50 a bottle.
/ 11 pm.

Crown & Goose NW1 £14 ★
100 Arlington Rd   0171-485 8008   8–3B
This Camden side street boozer was one of the first modishly revamped locals to have any gastronomic aspirations, and it still does what a gastropub ought to do – enjoyable, if not especially ambitious, cooking at reasonable prices. Your starter might be chicken and Parmesan salad (£4.95), followed by swordfish steak with salsa (£7). The house wine is £8 a bottle. / 10 pm; no credit cards.

Cucina NW3 £19* ★
45a South End Rd   0171-435 7814   8–2A
Particularly in culinarily challenged Hampstead, it's worth knowing about this bright modern British restaurant, near Belsize Park tube. As you might gather from house wine priced at £10.95 a bottle, though, you will have to tread pretty carefully to remain within our price limit, perhaps choosing the soup of the day (£3.95) followed by spinach and goat's cheese filo parcels (£9.50). / 10.30 pm, Fri & Sat 11 pm; closed Sun D; smart casual.

Da Mario SW7 £17 𝔸
15 Gloucester Rd   0171-584 9078   5–1B
Just around the corner from the Albert Hall, this lively pizzeria (a PizzaExpress in disguise) is a long-standing local favourite. Starters include pasta and bean soup with rocket (£4.20), and there's a good range of pizza and pasta dishes (£6-£7). House wine is £9.90 a bottle. (Though you couldn't really visit it on our budget, we should note that the rather sweaty basement disco makes a fun and relatively inexpensive party venue.) / 11.30 pm; no Switch; book for disco.

Da Pierino SW7 £14 ★
37 Thurloe Pl   0171-581 3770   5–2C
This laid-back, family-run Italian diner is a useful spot – just by South Kensington tube – for those wanting a serious refuel, and it is one of the few places locally where you can go pretty much the Full Monty, and keep within our budget. The speciality is pizzas (around £5), and house wine is £8.40 a bottle. / 11.15 pm; closed Mon; no Amex & no Switch.

Daphne NW1 £15 ★
83 Bayham St   0171-267 7322   8–3C
The contrast between this long-running Camden Greek and its more famous Chelsea ladies-who-lunch namesake could hardly be more stark. On the value front, though, there's no doubt that this unpretentious taverna is the one to prefer. Top bang for your buck is to be had from the 2-course lunch (£5.75) – you might try grilled halloumi, followed by afelia (pork in wine and coriander). Even in the evening, you'd have to stuff yourself to exceed our price limit. The house wine is £10.75 a litre. / 11.30 pm; closed Sun; no Amex.

Daquise SW7 £13 -
20 Thurloe St   0171-589 6117   5–2C
It's rather difficult to account for the affection in which this long-established Polish restaurant and tea room is held. Perhaps it's the convenient location, near the South Kensington museums. Perhaps it's the Warsaw-circa-1955 atmosphere. Unlikely that the food's the draw, though, even if it is inexpensive for the area. Soup (£2.50) followed by a potato pancake (£5.50) would be a typical budget choice, or, best of all go for a cup of afternoon tea (80p) and a cake (up to £2.50). / 10.45 pm; no Amex; no smoking area.

La Delizia £14 ★
246 Old Brompton Rd, SW5   0171-373 6085   5–2A
63-65 Chelsea Manor St, SW3   0171-376 4111   5–3C
Many Italians live around Chelsea, and most of them seem to hang out at the branches of this chic chain of pizzerias – at the Earl's Court branch, it's Italian football nights that really pack 'em in. As you might expect, pizzas (around £7) are generally good, as are pastas and salads, at about the same price. The house wine is £8.95 a bottle. As we go to press, the future of the Chelsea Farmer's Market branch (Sydney St, SW3 tel 0171-351 6701), which is currently closed, is very uncertain. / Midnight; no credit cards; no booking in summer.

Diwana Bhel-Poori House NW1 £9 ★
121 Drummond St   0171-387 5556   8–4C
For top value, visit this long-established veggie Indian near Euston at lunchtime, when there's a £4.95 buffet menu – to see what's on offer, check out the bowls in the window. Even à la carte, you would be hard-pushed to spend anything approaching our price-limit – for an evening visit, though, the rather sparse '60s surroundings may not be everyone's cup of tea. BYO. / 11.30 pm; no smoking area; Fri-Sun no booking.

don Fernando's TW9 £15 A
27f The Quadrant   0181-948 6447   1–4A
Lively, large tapas bar – just by Richmond station – which dishes up some of the better grub in the area. It's a fun place for a get-together – they do a generous set menu for £12.95 per person, minimum 4 people – or stick to the tapas, all priced at under a fiver. House Rioja is £9.75 a bottle, or buoy the party spirit with a jug of sangria (£9.50). / 11 pm; no Amex.

Don Pepe NW8 £14 A★
99 Frampton St   0171-262 3834   8–4A
The oldest tapas bar in town, near Lords, still makes a reliable choice. You can in fact dine in the restaurant within our budget at any time – the 3-course set menu is £13.95 – but it's much more fun to have tapas in the bar, especially when there's live music (most nights). The all-Hispanic wine list kicks off at £10.50 a bottle. / Midnight; closed Sun.

Dove W6 £11 A
19 Upper Mall   0181-748 5405   7–2B
This charming riverside pub at Hammersmith is popular on a sunny day, and it makes a cosy winter destination too. It's the setting which is the attraction, rather than the food, but the realisation of dishes such as Cajun chicken (£5.95), or steak and kidney pudding (£4.95) is perfectly competent. The house wine is £10 a bottle, or down a pint of ESB (£2.15). / 10 pm; no Amex; no booking.

The Eagle EC1 £16 A★
159 Farringdon Rd   0171-837 1353   9–1A
This converted Clerkenwell boozer may look unremarkable nowadays, but in the early '90s it broke the mould by demonstrating that it was quite possible to serve good food in a pub. Then as now, its inventive Mediterranean cooking really draws the crowds. The emphasis is on main course dishes – perhaps braised pork belly with onions and garlic potatoes (£8). There's a good selection of wines at relatively modest cost, starting at £9.50 a bottle. / 10.30 pm; closed Sun; no credit cards; no booking.

East One EC1 £18 A
175-179 St John St   0171-566 0088   9–1A
We're not huge fans of the places where you choose your own ingredients and then watch them being wokked up before your very eyes. This Smithfield spot is probably the best of them, however, and your £13.50 (lunch, £10) buys you unlimited stir-fry and as much boiled or fried rice as you can eat (or there's an à la carte menu, with main courses around the £6 mark). To maintain the party atmosphere, there's a long list of drinks, including house wine at a whopping £13.50 a bottle. / 11 pm; closed Sat L & Sun D.

Eat £ 6 -
3 Duke of York Street, SW1   0171-930 0960   3–3D
39 Villiers Street, WC2   0171-839 2282   4–4D
170 Fleet St, EC4   0171-583 2585   9–2A
It's very difficult not to compare this expanding quality sandwich, salads and coffee chain with its better established and more smartly decorated rival Pret A Manger. Standards are broadly similar – the sandwiches here seem less generously filled, but are, in some cases, more interesting. Coffee here's quite pricey (from £1.05), and sandwiches range from 99p to about £2.50, with cakes and desserts from £1. Solid soups (from £1.40) are a further attraction (although they charge a miserly 30p extra for bread). / 6pm, WC2 7.30 pm; no smoking; no booking

Eco SW4 £ 17 ★★
162 Clapham High St   0171-978 1108   10–2D
Good-quality, if not inexpensive pizzas (£6-£7), have helped to establish this large, reverberative Clapham site as one of the most wildly popular places south of the river, especially with trendier types. Culinary attractions also include starters such as marinated aubergine, roasted peppers and anchovies (£4.90) and salads (£8.50). The house wine is £9.75 a bottle. / 11 pm, Sat & Sun 11.30 pm; Mon-Fri only, no smoking area.

Ed's Easy Diner £ 10 -
12 Moor St, W1   0171-439 1955   4–2A
Trocadero, W1   0171-287 1951   3–3D
362 King's Rd, SW3   0171-352 1956   5–3B
16 Hampstead High St, NW3   0171-431 1958   8–1A
Perch on a stool at the long shiny counters of this all-American '50s-themed diner chain to enjoy hearty portions of classic burger-and-fries fare at reasonable prices. A cheeseburger and fries costs about £6. Wash it down with milkshakes at £2.50 or American beers from £2.85. / Midnight, Fri & Sat 1 am, W1 Sun 11 pm; no booking.

Efes Kebab House £ 18 -
1) 80 Great Titchfield St, W1   0171-636 1953   2–1B
2) 175-177 Gt Portland St, W1   0171-436 0600   2–1B
Established in 1972, this pair of Fitzrovia restaurants has long been a byword for reasonable value. If you avail yourself of the glitzier delights of Efes II, there's the added attraction of belly-dancing nightly, but both places offer the same menu of Turkish staples at good prices – meze (£3.75) followed by a mixed grill, including rice and salad (£8) would be typical. The places are 'naturals' for parties, but the set menus which are the obvious festive choice will lead you slightly outside our price bracket, even before you consume copious quantities of house wine at £8.90 a bottle. / 11.30 pm, Fri & Sat 3 am; 1) closed Sun.

Elistano SW3   £18   A★
25-27 Elystan St   0171-584 5248   5–2C
Even in pricey Chelsea, there are a few backwaters where you can find simple, good-value cooking. This one's been well and truly discovered by the locals, so it's best to book ahead if you want to enjoy the likes of baked aubergine with tomato and Parmesan (£4.90), followed by veal, artichokes and mushrooms (£9). Pastas (around £5) are a top price-conscious option. The house wine is £7.50 a bottle. / 11 pm; closed Sat L & Sun.

Emile's   £17   ★
144 Wandsworth Br Rd, SW6   0171-736 2418   10–1B
96-98 Felsham Rd, SW15   0181-789 3323   10–2B
This Fulham and Putney duo are always full — something to do with the lure of the consistently good-quality British food, in comfortable and homely surroundings. From the 2-course set menu (£13.50, always available), you could try Cheddar and herb soufflé, followed by an exemplary beef Wellington. A bottle of house wine is £10. / 11 pm; D only; closed Sun; no Amex.

Esarn Kheaw W12   £18   ★
314 Uxbridge Rd   0181-743 8930   7–1B
It's not any special charm (or particularly efficient service) which leads people to seek out this inconspicous Shepherd's Bush Thai, so it must have something to do with the quality of preparation of dishes such as home-made sausages with ginger and chilli (£3.85), followed, perhaps, by spiced duck, North Eastern style (£6.95). The house wine is £7.50 a bottle. / 11 pm; closed Sat L & Sun L; no Switch.

L'Estaminet WC2   £17*   ★
14 Garrick St   0171-379 1432   4–3C
If you're looking for a comfortable (if not wildly exciting) spot to dine pre-theatre, it's well worth bearing in mind the early-evening 2-course set menu (Mon-Thu £10.99, Fri & Sat £14.50) offered by this well-established, bourgeois French restaurant in Covent Garden — your choice might be prawn salad followed by monkfish, washed down with house wine at £9.90 a bottle. / 11 pm; closed Sun.

Il Falconiere SW7   £20   ★
84 Old Brompton Rd   0171-589 2401   5–2B
It may be in an idiom that's a bit dated, but this long-established South Kensington trattoria has a loyal following thanks to its warm welcome and good value. The 3-course set menus sit easily in our budget at lunch (£10), less so in the evening (£14.50). The house wine is £9.50 a bottle. / 11.45 pm; closed Sun.

Fat Boy's W4 £14 ★
10a Edensor Rd   0181-994 8089   10–1A
This unpretentious Chiswick diner is a friendly and very busy place, serving standard Thai fare, such as chicken satay (£4.25) followed by the likes of stir-fried pork with ginger and spring onion (£4.95). Wine is available, but the option to take your own helps to keep costs down. / 11 pm; closed Sat L; no credit cards.

Fats W9 £15 -
178 Shirland Rd   0171-289 3884   1–2B
If you really want the best value, you should take-away from this Cajun/Creole café in the outer fringes of Maida Vale. If, however, you decide to stay, and let yourself be enveloped by the smells and the soft reggae background music, you'll still get a good (if not bargain) deal. Main courses include the likes of chicken in coconut cream sauce (£6.95) and fish Creole (£7.50). You can BYO for £1 a head corkage.
/ 10.15 pm; closed Sun; no credit cards; no smoking.

Faulkner's E8 £14 ★★
424-426 Kingsland Rd   0171-254 6152   1–2D
This prominently located East End chippy has an outstanding reputation for the quality of its cooking (and, with cod 'n' chips at £6.60, it's not bargain basement prices which keep people coming back). If you're hungry, kick off your meal with home-made fishcakes (£1.30) or smoked salmon salad (£3.95). The house wine is £7.20 or you can BYO (£2.50 corkage). / 10 pm; no credit cards.

Ffiona's W8 £15 𝔸★
51 Kensington Ch St   0171-937 4152   5–1A
When you've had a hard day and all you want is traditional, wholesome home-cooking, this Kensington eatery fits the bill, and if you get there before 7.30pm you can enjoy three courses for £9.95. The menu changes daily and you might have soup followed by chicken and leek pie and then apple crumble. There's also a 3-course set Sunday lunch menu (£12.50). With the house wine at £9 a bottle, and most main courses about the same cost, you can also just about dine here à la carte within our price limit. / 11.30 pm; D only ; no Amex & no Cheques.

Fileric £5 ★
57 Old Brompton Rd, SW7   0171-584 2967   5–2C
French pâtisseries don't come much more authentic than this Gallic-run spot in South Kensington. Delights include éclairs (£1.30) and millefeuilles (£1.60), and savoury snacks such as quiches (£1.60). The excellent coffees start at 80p. There is also a sibling in Battersea (12 Queenstown Rd, SW8 tel 0171-720 4844). / 8 pm; no booking.

La Finca £14   A
96-98 Pentonville Rd, N1   0171-837 5387   8–3D
185 Kennington Ln, SE11   0171-735 1061   10–1D
Especially in the thinly served areas of Kennington and King's Cross, these large and boisterous tapas bars are well worth knowing about. Standard tapas dishes cost £3-£4 each and the house wine is £8.95 a bottle. On Sundays, feast on paella for £5.95, washed down with a jug of sangria for the same price. / 11.15 pm; Fri & Sat N1 1.30 am, SE11 11.30 pm.

Florians N8 £14*   A
4 Topsfield Parade   0181-348 8348   1–1C
Frankly, it's the buzzy bar scene which is the particular attraction of this Hornsey Italian. On the food front, you'll find starters such as tomato and basil gnocchi (£3.50), and main courses including Italian sausage (£5.25). The restaurant at the rear is not so exciting, and not really in our price-range à la carte, but bear in mind that until 9pm it offers a 2-course set menu for £9.95 – perhaps rocket salad followed by chicken with root vegetables. The house wine is £9.50 a bottle. / 10.45 pm; no Amex.

Food for Thought WC2 £10   A★
31 Neal St   0171-836 0239   4–2C
Even carnivores are happy to brave the wooden staircase down to this cramped, cave-like north-Covent Garden basement. It's a laid-back spot, offering an eclectic range of inexpensive and wholesome veggie fare, such as Thai noodles with vegetables (£3.30) and quiches and salads (both from £2.60). There's also a mouth-watering selection of cakes and puddings, perhaps banana and strawberry scrunch (£2.70). BYO – no corkage. / 8.15 pm, Sun 3.45 pm; no credit cards; no smoking; no booking.

Formula Veneta SW10 £18*   A
14 Hollywood Rd   0171-352 7612   5–3B
Located not far from the Fulham Road, this attractive, modern trattoria attracts quite a trendy following. To keep within our budget, choose one of the antipasti dishes (around £6), and follow it with pasta – the speciality is fettucini in sausage and wild mushroom sauce, £6.25. The house wine is £10 a bottle. / 11.15 pm; closed Sun.

Fox & Anchor EC1 £14 A★
115 Charterhouse St   0171-253 4838   9–1B
It is fervently to be hoped that the days of our bizarre licensing laws are truly numbered. For the moment, though, this is one of the very few places in town where you can kick the day off with anything stronger than an orange juice, being one of the Smithfield Market pubs where those "on market business" – which seems to be rather loosely interpreted – can kick the day off with a huge meaty breakfast (£7), washed down with a pint of Tetley's (£2.20). At lunchtime, you might have a hearty steak and kidney pie (£7). The house wine is £8.50 a bottle. / 11 pm; closed Sat L (but open Sat bkfast) & Sun.

The Fox Reformed N16 £18 A
176 Stoke Newington Ch St   0171-254 5975   1–1C
There's nothing startling about this Stoke Newington wine bar, but its homely charm is part of the appeal. Many of the dishes are what you might call comforting – say, chicken liver parfait on melba toast (£4.25), followed by steamed cod on spinach with chive sauce (£8). The house wine is £8.75 a bottle, and there's a fair selection for not very much more. There is a nice, if small, rear garden for sunny days. / 10.30 pm.

Francofill SW7 £17 ★
1 Old Brompton Rd   0171-584 0087   5–2C
This modestly priced, but quite chic French bistro has recently been given a face-lift and a bar has been added. It remains one of the more affordable options in South Kensington. You might start with duck pâté and brioche (£4.50), followed by courgette and aubergine stew (£6.25) or goat's cheese salad (£7.50). The house wine is £10 a bottle. / 11 pm; no smoking area.

Frederick's N1 £19* A★
106 Camden Pas   0171-359 2888   8–3D
This large and attractive Islington restaurant (with its impressive rear conservatory) looks much too grand to be included in this book, so you feel you're getting a real bargain if you seek out the lunchtime or pre-theatre (in by 7pm, out by 8pm) options. In either case, your selection from the 2-course menu (£12) might be, say, parsnip soup followed by beef stroganoff. The house wine is £10 a bottle. / 11.30 pm; closed Sun; smart casual; no smoking area.

Frocks E9 £19* 🅐
95 Lauriston Rd   0181-986 3161   1–2D
One of the few East End places with any real reputation, this cosy English bistro is located near Victoria Park. A la carte, it falls just outside our budget, but the weekend breakfasts for which it is most famous (11am-4pm, around £5), and set lunches fall easily within it. A 3-course lunch will set you back £13 – you might have chicken livers on toasted brioche, followed by sausage and mash, with plum and walnut crumble for pudding. The house wine is £9.50 a bottle. / 11 pm; closed Sun D; no Sunday bookings.

Front Page SW3 £17 🅐
35 Old Church St   0171-352 2908   5–3C
This tastefully transformed panelled boozer, in a charming Chelsea back street, attracts a fashionable younger crowd. The food has no great pretensions, but it's enjoyable, solid stuff, such as chicken liver salad (£4.45) followed by linguine with rocket and pesto (£6.95). House wines kick off at £10 a bottle, or you could opt for a pint of bitter (£1.70). / 10 pm; no booking.

Fryer's Delight WC1 £5 ★★
19 Theobald's Rd   0171-405 4114   2–1D
Inexpensive chippies don't come more 'Central Castings' perfect than this Formica-and-fluorescent-strip Bloomsbury parlour, and it offers what in our view is probably the best value eat-in food to be had in central London. With cod 'n' chips at £3.80 and a mug of tea at 35p, you really can have a filling one-course meal here, and still have change from a fiver. No puddings. / 10 pm; no credit cards.

Futures EC2 £9 -
2 Exchange Sq   0171-638 6341   9–1D
Bright, almost glitzy Broadgate bar/restaurant which eschews veggie cliché and is very popular with those who work in the shiny offices which surround it. Two courses will set you back £8 – you might have soup followed by the quiche of the day, or a salad. In the evening, the bar element predominates, and you can sustain yourself on the likes of pizza fingers (£2.95). The house wine is £9.95 a bottle. / L only; closed Sat & Sun; no credit cards; no smoking except bkfast.

Futures EC3 £ 7 ★
8 Botolph Alley   0171-623 4529   9–3C
We don't generally include take-aways, but we've always had a soft spot for this smart City vegetarian, hidden away in the lanes near the Monument. Good food is hard enough to find in that part of town, and the nosh here really is better than at most of the places where they sit you down with a knife and fork! Soups (£1.90), salads (£2.80) and bakes (£3.60) are the sort of dishes which attract regular lunchtime queues. Top-quality, if not inexpensive, breakfasting fare is also available. / L only; closed Sat & Sun; no credit cards.

Galicia W10 £17 -
323 Portobello Rd   0181-969 3539   6–1A
Benefiting from the proximity of one of London's largest Hispanic communities, this North Kensington tapas bar is strong on authenticity – including service which can tend to grumpy – and high on atmosphere. The tapas (mostly £2.50-£5), washed down by house wine at a modest £7 a bottle, can be pretty good, too. / 11.30 pm; closed Mon.

Gastro SW4 £16 A★
67 Venn St   0171-627 0222   10–2D
This Gallic café/bistro in Clapham (opposite the Picture House) really is an all-day sort of place, equally suited to a coffee (£1) and a croissant (65p) as to a candlelit dinner. At dinner-time, expect real country cooking, and authentically hearty fare – perhaps crab soup (£4.25) and grilled tripe sausage with thyme (£7.45). A half-litre carafe of wine is £5.95. / Midnight; no credit cards; no smoking area; only groups of 15+.

The Gate W6 £17 ★★
51 Queen Caroline St   0181-748 6932   7–2C
Discerning veggies (and even some would-be converts) make the trek to this obscurely located spot, off a church courtyard near the Hammersmith roundabout. The attraction is some of the most consistently delicious meatless cooking in town, such as plantain fritters with sweet chilli sauce (£4.90) and fresh pasta with wild mushrooms and ricotta (£6.90). The house wine is £8.90 a bottle. / 10.45 pm; closed Sat L & Sun L.

El Gaucho SW3 £16 -
Chelsea Farmers' Mkt, 125 Sydney St   0171-376 8514   5–3C
A shack adjoining a garden centre might seem an odd location for an Argentinean restaurant, but that's done little to diminish the appeal of this Chelsea spot – especially on a sunny day, when you can sit on benches outside. Start with the likes of baked red peppers (£2.20), followed by char-grilled strip-loin (£9.90) and chips (£2.20). Given that you have to BYO, the corkage charge of £1.50 seems high. / 11 pm; no credit cards.

Geale's W8   £15   ★
2 Farmer St   0171-727 7969   6–2B
Nowadays, the local estate agents have given the name of Highgate Village to this chichi collection of houses just behind Notting Hill Gate. Geale's – west London's most famous chippy by far – predates this gentrification by a long way, though, and still looks like a cross between a '50s tearoom and a greasy spoon. Cod 'n' chips will set you back £8.50, washed down by house wine at a modest £6.25 a bottle.
/ 11 pm; closed Mon & Sun.

Geeta NW6   £12   ★
59 Willesden Ln   0171-624 1713   1–1B
It's what you might politely call 'nothing to look at', but this Kilburn café maintains its loyal following by offering very tasty south Indian cuisine at very modest cost – starters rarely cost more than £2, veggie curries are generally around the £3 mark, and meat curries a little more. The house wine is £6.50 a bottle. / 10.30 pm, Fri & Sat 11.30 pm; no Switch.

Ghillies   £18   ★
271 New King's Rd, SW6   0171-371 0434   10–1B
20 Bellevue Rd, SW17   0181-767 1858   10–2C
Though its pretensions seem no higher than your typical younger-scene bistro, the culinary standards of this mini-chain are higher than average. Carnivores are catered for, but fish is the speciality, so go for something like Cajun spiced tiger prawns (£5.25), followed by fishcakes (£7.95). House wines start at £8.95 a bottle. / 10.45 pm.

Golden Dragon W1   £16   ★
28-29 Gerrard St   0171-734 2763   4–3A
If you revel in a hectic atmosphere, this party-style Chinatown spot, with dragons glaring at you from every corner, may be for you. Set meals, starting at £10.50 a head, are the cheapest budget option, but, à la carte, most main dishes are little more than £6. The house wine is £8.50 a bottle.
/ 11.30 pm, Fri & Sat midnight.

Good Earth SW3   £15*   A★
233 Brompton Rd   0171-584 3658   5–2C
Knightsbridge offers rather thin pickings to the budget diner, so it's particularly worth knowing about this smart and comfortable oriental. It's out of our price-range in the evening, but at lunchtime choose between a 2-course set lunch (£9.95) or – a new possibility – a one-plate Japanese noodle ('ramen') dish for about the same price. The house wine is £10 a bottle. / 11 pm.

Gopal's of Soho W1 £18 ★
12 Bateman St   0171-434 1621   4–2A
One of the very best bets for a West End Indian, this smartly conventional curry house offers dishes both familiar (say, chicken tikka masala, £6.25) and less so, such as crab stewed in coconut, £4.60, or curried halibut steamed in a leaf, £8.50. The house wine is £8.50 a bottle. / 11.15 pm; smart casual.

Gordon's Wine Bar WC2 £10   Ⓐ
47 Villiers St   0171-930 1408   4–4D
If it's Olde London character you're after, you won't do any better than this wonderfully scruffy wine bar, a few paces from Embankment tube. It's tremendously popular, thanks to its atmosphere and the reasonable price of both food and drink. Wines start from £8.25 a bottle (with plenty of choice for a couple of pounds more) and the good, basic food includes well-kept cheeses, salads and hot dishes of the day – all priced in the £4-£7 range. / 9 pm; closed Sat L & Sun; no Amex; no booking.

Gourmet Pizza Company £15 ★
7-9 Swallow St, W1   0171-734 5182   3–3D
Gabriels Whf, 56 Upper Ground, SE1   0171-928 3188   9–3A
18 Mackenzie Walk, E14   0171-345 9192   1–3D
It's a pity there aren't more of these innovative pizzerias. They offer some quite good starters (perhaps avocado, pine kernels and mixed leaf salad, £3.40), but the main attractions are the weird and wonderful pizzas such as English Breakfast (£6.25) and Thai Chicken (£7.75). The house wine is £9.95 a bottle. The Gabriel's Wharf branch has outside seating and a fantastic riverside setting. / 10.45 pm; W1 & E14, no smoking area; need 8+ to book.

Goya SW1 £15   -
34 Lupus St   0171-976 5309   2–4C
Pimlico is thinly provided with good places to eat, inexpensive or otherwise, so it's worth knowing about this jolly tapas bar, which tends to attract a younger crowd – especially on a warm day, when you can sit outside. All the usual tapas are available, mostly in the £2.50-£5 range, and the house wine is £9 a bottle. There's a restaurant in the basement, but it's less of an attraction. / 11.30 pm; no smoking area.

Granita N1 £17* ★
127 Upper St   0171-226 3222   8–2D
This sparse, but much-lauded modern British restaurant in Islington offers an opportunity for budget diners to sample its delights with excellent value set lunches (two courses, £11.95). Your choice might include five-spiced chicken spring rolls or char-grilled tuna with chick pea salad, followed by ginger and honey ice cream. The house wine is £10.50 a bottle. / 10.30 pm; closed Mon & Tue L; no Amex & no Switch.

Great Nepalese NW1 £13 ★
48 Eversholt St   0171-388 6737   8–3C
The popularity of this long-serving Euston-side Indian belies its inauspicious location. The simplest choice is a Nepalese set lunch or dinner (curry, pilau rice, relishes and dessert for £11.75), but, especially in a group, there are lots of interesting dishes to sample which will still leave you comfortably within our price limit, and the staff offer friendly and helpful advice. The house wine is £7.25 a bottle.
/ 11.30 pm; no Switch.

Greek Valley NW8 £16 -
130 Boundary Rd   0171-624 3217   8–3A
There's nothing cutting-edge about the cooking at this long-established, family-run Greek taverna in St John's Wood, but it's welcoming and reasonably priced – most starters, such as meatballs, are £2.50, and main courses, including moussaka, are £6.75. The house wine is £7.50 a bottle.
/ Midnight; D only; closed Sun; no Amex.

Grenadier SW1 £ 5 𝔸
18 Wilton Rw   0171-235 3074   2–3A
You won't be able to accommodate within our budget a meal in the tiny rear dining room of this mega-cute pub, located in a charming cobbled Belgravia mews. The place makes a characterful choice for a bar snack, though – you might have a burger, a club sandwich or salmon fishcakes (all £5.75). Cognoscenti, however, head for a sausage (£1) washed down with a Bloody Mary (£4.25), for both of which the place is famous. / 9.45 pm.

Gresslin's NW3 £17* ★★
13 Heath St   0171-794 8386   8–2A
The quality of the cooking at this modern British restaurant would make it notable anywhere but – in the culinary desert of downtown Hampstead – its survival is remarkable. The place is out of our price-bracket in the evening, but the 2-course lunch – perhaps goat's cheese salad followed by chicken with stir-fry vegetables – comes in at a bargain £7.95, washed down by house wine at £9.95 a bottle. The 2-course Sunday lunch, at £13.95, would also just squeeze into our price-range. / 10.45 pm; closed Mon L & Sun D; no Amex; no smoking area.

Gung-Ho NW6 £19* 𝔸★
330-332 West End Ln   0171-794 1444   1–1B
West Hampstead's best kept local secret is this stylish, welcoming and popular Chinese. You will have to choose reasonably economically to stay within our price limit – you might have a mixed selection of starters (£12 for two) followed by sweet and sour chicken (£5.20) with special noodles (£4.50). House wine is £9.60 a bottle. / 11.30 pm.

Halepi W2 £18 -
18 Leinster Ter   0171-262 1070   6–2C
As house wine at £12.50 a bottle suggests, this homely-looking taverna just north of Hyde Park is not quite as inexpensive a venue as its appearance might suggest. The starters, such as taramasalata (£3.25) offer the best value, as meaty main courses run around the £10 mark. / 12.30 am.

Hamine W1 £12 ★
84 Brewer St   0171-439 0785   3–2D
This was one of the first Japanese noodle bars in London – it offers quick service and authentic cooking, and still attracts an encouragingly oriental clientèle. It's perhaps most worth knowing about as one of the best late-night pit stops in the West End. The best value option is the set menu – £7.50 buys you a noodle dish (with a topping of your choice), chicken fried rice and shrimps. A glass of house wine is £2.50, or saki for a pound more. / 2.30 am, Sat 1.30 am, Sun midnight; no credit cards; no booking.

Harbour City W1 £18 -
46 Gerrard St   0171-439 7859   4–3B
The décor may be rather understated by local standards, but this Chinatown spot still attracts a faithful following. It's at lunchtime that people seek the place out for it's notably interesting selection of dim sum, when nothing costs more than £2.80. At other times, you'd be wise, to remain within our budget, to stick to the more conventional options such as sweet and sour pork (£5.50). House wine is £8 a bottle.
/ 11.15 pm, Fri & Sat 11.45 pm.

Hard Rock Café W1 £17 𝔸
150 Old Park Ln   0171-629 0382   3–4B
The West End has been besieged in recent years by theme diners (some of the more egregious examples of which have, mercifully, recently closed). None of them has yet matched the consistency and charm of the original, still decorated with its rock memorabilia and still pumping out loud rock music all day long. You wouldn't expect it to be cheap – onion rings are £3.95 and a burger is £8.25 – but prices are reasonable for a place which is an obligatory stop on many tourist itineraries. The house wine is £8.95 a bottle, or there's a good range of American bottled beers (£2.55). / 12.30 am, Fri & Sat 1 am; no Switch; no smoking area; no booking.

Havana W1 £18 -
17 Hanover Sq   0171-629 2552   3–1C
This explicitly isn't a foodie recommendation, but younger souls looking for a fun night out in the West End could do much worse than this Cuban-themed Mayfair joint. It's decorated in a louche nightclub style (making much use of fake leopard-skin) and there's frequently live music. Sustain yourself with tapas (around £3.50), substantial salads (£6.25) or charcoal grills (around £9). The house wine is £9.65 a bottle. / 11.45 pm.

The Havelock Tavern W14 £18 ★
57 Masbro Rd   0171-603 5374   7–1C
Olympia and Shepherd's Bush are a major centre of London's gastropub revolution. This is one of its leaders, offering good quality modern British cooking in pleasant surroundings. You might have warm smoked herring salad with mustard dressing (£5) followed by roast rump of beef with chips (£9.50), washed down by house wine at £9 a bottle. Arrive early, especially at weekends. / 10 pm, Sun 9.30 pm; no credit cards; no booking.

Heather's SE8 £14 ★
74 McMillan St   0181-691 6665   1–3D
Those prepared to make the pilgrimage to this vast veggie in a converted Bermondsey boozer are rewarded in summer by a nice garden, and all year by inexpensive and tasty vegetarian fare from an extensive buffet (£12). Its range might include the likes of roast pumpkin and garlic soup or Thai chick-pea and coconut curry. The house wine, organic of course, is £7.50 a bottle. / 11 pm, 9 pm Sun; closed Mon; no credit cards; no smoking.

Helter Skelter SW9 £19 ★
50 Atlantic Rd   0171-274 8600   10–2D
This informal Brixton restaurant serves up good-quality modern British cooking at reasonable prices. You might start with the likes of asparagus in puff pastry with Stilton sauce £4.80, followed by Thai chicken curry (£8.80) or feta, spinach and pine nut filo parcels with pumpkin ragú (£9.20). The house wine is £9.50 a bottle. / 11 pm, Fri & Sat 11.30 pm; D only.

Hodgson's Wine Bar WC2 £15 -
115 Chancery Ln   0171-404 5027   2–2D
It may be culinarily undramatic, but this rather old-fashioned basement wine bar offers a useful and quite inexpensive rendezvous in the thinly provided area around the Inns of Court. Salads are around £3.75 and a meaty main course, perhaps a minute steak, would set you back £7.50. The house wine is £8.95 a bottle. / 10 pm.

Home EC1 £19* 🅐★
100-106 Leonard St   0171-684 8618   9–1D
Even by the standards of hyper-trendy Hoxton, this basement bar-restaurant is pretty cool. Perhaps surprisingly, the imaginative and tasty grub served in the restaurant is an attraction in itself – chicken liver parfait (£4), followed by Cornish mussels in green coconut broth (£8.50) would be typical choices from the lunch menu – in the evenings, the food is both more ambitious and more expensive, although still generally within our price range. House wine is £8.50 a bottle, or swig bottled beers from £2.40. / 10 pm; closed Sat L & Sun; no Amex.

The Honest Cabbage SE1 £17 ★
99 Bermondsey Street   0171-234 0080   9–4D
Across the road from Bermondsey antiques market, this newly converted pub has brought interesting and ambitious modern British fare to a thin area. There is a daily-changing menu which might include wild mushroom soup (£3), followed by Caesar salad with grilled mackerel (£9). House wine at £10 a bottle is pretty pricey, considering. / 10 pm; closed Sun D; no Amex.

Hope & Sir Loin EC1 £17 A★
94 Cowcross St   0171-253 8525   9–1B
The upstairs dining room of this well-known Smithfield pub is one of the hallowed few where you can kick off the day with a full (and we mean full) English breakfast (£7.50), washed down, legally, with a pint of Guinness (£2.60). At lunchtime, you might have a rib-eye steak (£10.95), with house red at £11.95 a bottle. / L only; closed Sat & Sun.

Hornimans SW4 £15 -
69 Clapham Common S'side   0181-673 9162   10–2D
This jolly common-side Clapham restaurant is particularly popular with the younger souls thereabouts, and it's a relaxing place to enjoy food that doesn't try too hard – perhaps goat's cheese to start (£3.50) followed by pan-fried duck with honey and vanilla sauce (£8.95). The house wine is £8.95 a bottle. / 11 pm; D only; no Amex.

Hujo's W1 £19 A★
11 Berwick St   0171-734 5144   3–2D
This is one of the incredibly few genuine bistros (still less modern British bistros) anywhere near the centre of town, and it's worth braving the sleazy environs of Berwick Street market to try it out. Wild mushrooms with new potatoes and walnuts (£5.25) would be a typical starter, and then you might have grilled smoked salmon steak (£ 8.75). House wine is £8.25 a bottle. / Midnight; closed Sun.

Hunan SW1 £18* ★★
51 Pimlico Rd   0171-730 5712   5–2D
The rather grotty exterior belies one of the best and most welcoming Chinese restaurants in town – this quirky, family-run spot has been something of a Pimlico secret for many years now. Budget diners will have to take some care to keep the bill within our limit, but it is possible if you have a starter like crispy prawn toast (£6), followed by pork with hot spicy sauce (£5.50). The house wine is £10 a bottle.
/ 11.15 pm; closed Sun; no Switch.

Ikkyu £18 ★
67 Tottenham Ct Rd, W1   0171-636 9280   2–1C
7 Newport Pl, WC2   0171-439 3554   4–3B
The original (W1) branch of this Japanese chain has long been reputed for offering top value. Its offshoot may not offer quite such a bargain, but it does have a rather more generally accessible location, on the fringes of Chinatown. A large platter of sushi (14 pieces) will set you back £11.50, or you could have a dish like seafood noodles (£6.50), with a glass of saki (£2.40). / 10.30 pm, WC2 Fri & Sat 11.30 pm; W1, closed Sat & Sun L; W1 no Switch, WC2 no Amex; WC2 no smoking area.

The Imperial Arms SW6 £15 -
577 King's Rd   0171-736 8549   5–4A
A minimalist revamp and dim lighting have improved the atmosphere at this Fulham-fringe boozer, whose ambitious modern British menu is competently realised. Your meal might combine chicken liver pâté and red onion marmalade (£3.75) with spinach, mushroom and Cheddar strudel (£4.95). There are some good beers – Imperial Best is £2.30 a pint – or a bottle of the house wine is £9.90. / 9.30 pm; closed Sat D.

Inaho W2 £19* ★★
4 Hereford Rd   0171-221 8495   6–1B
Some of the very best inexpensive Japanese food in town is to be had at this tiny Bayswater café. The set lunches are, of course, the top-value option – the £10 beef teriyaki menu, for example, also includes an appetizer, soup, rice and fruit. A la carte, the same sum would, for example, buy you assorted sushi pieces. House wine is £7.50 a bottle. / 11 pm; closed Sat L & Sun; no Amex & no Switch.

India Club WC2 £11 -
143 Strand   0171-836 0650   2–2D
Some say that its standards are not what they were, but the utter budgetness, the quintessential economicality of this quirky '50 institution, on the first floor of a nondescript hotel near the Aldwych, makes it a 'must' for this guide. Curries are around a fiver, and you keep prices down by bringing your own booze. / 10 pm; closed Sun; no credit cards; need 6+ to book.

Indian Ocean SW17 £15 ★
216 Trinity Rd   0181-672 7740   10–2C
Not far from Wandsworth Common, this smart curry house is above-average in both food and service. Standard curries are around a fiver, with the seafood specialities rather more, and the house wine is £6.75 a bottle. The Sunday afternoon buffet offers fair value, at £7.95 a head. / 11.30 pm.

Isfehan W2 £18 -
3-4 Bouverie Pl   0171-460 1030   6–1D
If you're looking for late-night jollity in the somewhat grim purlieus of Paddington Station, seek out this pullulating Persian, which boasts live music four times weekly. With house wine at £8.95 a bottle and all starters at £2.95, you could have a top-of-the-market main course, such as mixed seafood kebab (£11.95), and still stay within our budget. / Midnight.

Ishbilia SW1 £17* -
9 William St   0171-235 7788   2–3A
This smart, family-run Lebanese establishment has the twin virtues of being quite authentic (as the largely Arabic clientèle suggests) and of offering reasonable-value light meals in pricey Knightsbridge. To keep costs down, you could make a meal of starters, such as houmous (£3), tabbouleh (£4) and aubergine salad (£4), or a main course, such as minced lamb with yoghurt and pine nuts, would set you back around a tenner. The house wine is £9.50 a bottle. / Midnight; no Switch.

Italian Kitchen WC2 £18 ★
17-21 Tavistock St   0171-379 9696   4–3D
This unpretentious Italian bistro near the British Museum (and convenient for the northern part of Theatreland) always strikes us as what an inexpensive restaurant should be — unpretentious, adequately comfortable (and no more) and with the emphasis on the cooking. If you're really saving the pennies, get there by 7pm for the (unambitious) two-course menu of the day (£4.95). A la carte, prices vary quite widely, but if you choose with care you can stay within our price limit . The house wines start at £9.95 a bottle. / Midnight; no booking Fri & Sat.

Iznik N5 £15   𝔸★
19 Highbury Pk   0171-354 5697   8–2D
It's not just good Turkish cooking that makes this one of the top budget places in town — its interior verges on kitsch, but manages to achieve a magic matched by few establishments, even some that charge very much more. Most starters are around the £3 mark, and a typical main course would be chicken in pepper and mustard sauce (£6.50). The house wine is £7.95 a bottle. / 11 pm; no Amex.

Jenny Lo's Teak House SW1 £11 -
14 Eccleston St   0171-259 0399   2–4B
Jenny Lo is the daughter of Britain's most prolific Chinese cookery writer and this stylish oriental noodle bar near Victoria Station is on the site of her father's cookery school. Noodles, noodles and more noodles are the basic culinary proposition, with most dishes around the £7 mark. Accompany the dishes with a range of therapeutic teas, or the house wine at £9.50 a bottle. / 10 pm; closed Sun; no credit cards; no booking.

Joy King Lau W1   £14   ★
3 Leicester St   0171-437 1132   4–3A
This large Chinatown establishment is distinguished by very good cooking and (unusually for the area) a friendly welcome. Lunchtime is a good time to visit for the notable dim sum – most dishes cost between £1.70-£2.80. The à la carte is also well realised, with most main dishes costing about £5.50. House wine is £7.50 a bottle, or economise with tea (60p).
/ 11.30 pm; no Switch.

Kalamaras, Micro W2   £16   ★
66 Inverness Mews   0171-727 5082   6–2C
It may now lack both a big brother (Mega K closed some time ago) and the celebrity it once enjoyed, but this unpretentious Greek, in an obscure mews location, just off Queensway, is still worth knowing about. Prices are kept down by the BYO policy (no beer), so you can push the boat out and still stay within our price limit. You might start with deep-fried squid (£4.50), with stifado (veal casserole with shallots, £7.90) as the main course. / 11 pm; D only; no Switch.

Kastoori SW17   £11   ★★
188 Upper Tooting Rd   0181-767 7027   10–2C
Top-quality Indain/East African vegetarian cooking has for many years won a disproportionate reputation for this unassuming, family-run Tooting spot. All dishes are under a fiver, and there's an unusually good range of wines, kicking off at £7.50 a bottle / 10.30 pm; closed Mon L & Tue L; no Amex & no Switch.

Kavanagh's N1   £16*   ★
26 Penton St   0171-833 1380   8–3D
A la carte, you would probably exceed our price limit at this bright and quirky modern British restaurant in Islington. If you stick to the 2-course set menu (£10.95), however, you will stay comfortably within it – your choice might be hot smoked haddock followed by char-grilled swordfish with aubergines and chilli dressing. The house wine is £9.20 a bottle.
/ 10.30 pm; closed Mon & Sat L & Sun D; no Amex.

Khan's W2   £11   ★
13-15 Westbourne Grove   0171-727 5420   6–1C
Being large and giving a (misleading) impression of disorganisation, this famous Bayswater curry house invariably attracts comparisons with the subcontinent itself, or at least with, say, Bombay railway station. These parallels are certainly apt, but what keeps people coming back is fairly good food at very reasonable prices – most main dishes are £4 or less, and the house wine is £6.75 a bottle. / 11.45 pm.

Khan's of Kensington SW7   £15   ★
3 Harrington Rd   0171-581 2900   5–2B
Modern, if not super-stylish, this South Kensington Indian offers reliable curries (around £6.50) of an above-average standard, and house wine at a reasonable £7.95 a bottle. If a couple can't decide what to choose, there's a 4-course menu for £33.95, which would lead to a total bill just outside our price-limit. / 11.15 pm, Fri & Sat 11.45 pm; no smoking area.

King's Road Café SW3   £16   -
208 King's Rd   0171-351 6645   5–3C
Chelsea's King's Road may be one of the capital's longest-established promenades, but it offers precious few places to stop off for a light meal. This one, on the airy first floor of the Habitat shop, offers a useful range of light dishes (mainly of Mediterranean inspiration), including a fair selection for vegetarians. A 2-course menu (£8.90) is generally available, with house wine at £11.50 a bottle. Good cakes (£2.60) are an attraction at off-peak times. / open shop hours only, with L till 5 pm; L only; no Amex; no smoking area.

Krungtap SW10   £14   -
227 Old Brompton Rd   0171-259 2314   5–2A
After a fire-induced closure, this popular Thai restaurant in Earl's Court has reopened in a brighter, but less characterful format. It still offers quite tasty dishes at reasonable prices – there's a 3-course lunch menu for £4.90, or you can dine à la carte at modest cost. House wine is £6.50 a bottle. / 10.30 pm; D only; no Amex; no smoking area.

Kulu Kulu W1   £13   ★
76 Brewer St   0171-734 7316   3–2D
The attention is focused on the food at this dependable Soho Japanese café which is rather less hi-tech and flashy in style than other West End conveyor-belt sushi bars. The plates range from £1.20 to £3, noodle dishes start at £2.40 and the tea is free. / 10 pm; closed Sun; no Amex; no booking.

The Ladbroke Arms W11   £18   ★
54 Ladbroke Rd   0171-727 6648   6–2B
The food may be fairly traditional in inspiration, but its aspirations are much higher than average at this smart boozer, just off Notting Hill Gate. If you're hungry, you might have chicken-liver pâté (£4.95) before, say, roast guinea fowl with cranberry and red wine sauce (£8.95). Drink house wine at £9.75 a bottle, or Best Bitter at £2.10 a pint. In summer, the outside tables fill up early. / 9.45 pm; no Amex; book L only.

Lahore Kebab House E1 £10 ★★
2 Umberston St   0171-488 2551   1–2D
Famous for its cooking, infamous for its décor (lack of) and service (ditto), this East End institution leaves few indifferent. The emphasis is on top quality meat at bargain prices – perhaps Karahi lamb (£4.50) – and prices are kept low by the BYO policy. / 11.45 pm; no credit cards.

Lansdowne NW1 £17 𝔸
90 Gloucester Ave   0171-483 0409   8–3B
The bright and cheerful ambience of this Primrose Hill gastropub is perhaps a greater strength than its cooking, but it's a useful place to know about for a meal of, say, soup (£3.50) followed by grilled squid with rocket and red pepper salsa (£8.50). The house wine is £8.50 a bottle. / 10 pm; closed Mon L; no Amex; book Sun L only.

La Lanterna SE1 £17 -
6–8 Mill Street   0171-252 2420   1–3D
There's not much in way of quality, inexpensive eating in the southerly environs of Tower Bridge, which makes this unpretentious Italian worth knowing about. Starters are relatively pricey, with the likes of deep-fried Mozzarella at £5.75, so you may want to stick to a pizza or pasta dish (all around the £7 mark), and follow with crème caramel (£3.50). The house wine is £9.25 a bottle. / 11 pm; closed Sat L.

Latymers W6 £11 ★
157 Hammersmith Rd   0181-741 2507   7–2C
A gin palace near the Hammersmith roundabout may seem an unlikely foodie recommendation, but the rear dining room has a justified reputation for the quality of its Thai fare. The 'Quick Lunch' – one-plate dishes such as pad thai or green chicken curry with rice (£4.55) – are the top-value choice. Even in the evening, however – with starters, such as beef satay, at £2.95, and main courses just over a fiver – you'll hardly break the bank. The house wine is £9.20 a bottle. / 10 pm; closed Sun; no Switch; no booking at lunch.

Launceston Place W8 £20* 𝔸★★
1a Launceston Pl   0171-937 6912   5–1B
This celebrated Kensington restaurant, tucked away behind Gloucester Road, offers the budget diner a chance to taste the imaginative modern British fare (but only just within budget). Between 7pm and 8pm, the 2-course prix fixe menu will set you back £14.50 – you might try roast guinea fowl with cep mushrooms, followed by twice-baked chocolate souffle. House wine is £10.75 a bottle. (The late supper menu, for which we used to feature this establishment, is sadly no more.) / 11.30 pm; closed Sat L & Sun D.

Laurent NW2   £16   ★★
428 Finchley Rd   0171-794 3603   1–1B
If you like couscous, it's worth the trip to Cricklewood to seek out this unpretentious café, which has established a big reputation on the basis of one starter, brik à l'oeuf (£2.65), and couscous five ways (£7-£11.50). House vino starts at £9 a bottle – there's an interesting list of North Africans, if you fancy going native. / 11 pm; closed Sun; no Switch.

Lavender   £17   𝔸★
171 Lavender Hill, SW11   0171-978 5242   10–2C
24 Clapham Rd, SW9   0171-793 0770   10–1D
These friendly, informal local bistros are of the type we hope to see more of over coming years – simple and good-value places, serving unpretentious modern British fare from an ever-changing blackboard menu. Pine nut and pesto salad (£3.75) is the sort of starter which you might expect, with, for a main course, roast fennel and ricotta tart with salsa (£7.20). The house wine is £7.95 a bottle. / 11 pm.

Leadenhall Tapas Bar EC3   £14   -
27 Leadenhall Mkt   0171-623 1818   9–2D
Much of the fare is so far removed from Spain that the name is almost a misnomer, but this wine bar, with intriguing views down on to Leadenhall Market, still makes a pleasant City rendezvous. The tapas menu includes all the usual suspects – chorizo, tortillas, olives – as well as some good English cheeses, with most items costing £3-£5. The (French) house wine is £9.50 a bottle. / 9 pm; closed Sat & Sun; need 6+ to book.

Lemonia NW1   £17   𝔸★
89 Regent's Pk Rd   0171-586 7454   8–3B
Big, buzzy and perennially welcoming, this super-scale Primrose Hill taverna is one of north London's most consistent success-stories. The top-value meal is the 3-course set lunch (£7.95), but even in the evening, with starters such as fried baby squid (£4.25) and main courses such as dolmades (£7.50), you can keep within our price-limit. The house wine is £10.50 a litre. / 11.30 pm; closed Sat L & Sun D; no Amex.

Leonardo's SW10   £17*   ★
397 King's Rd   0171-352 4146   5–3B
This traditional, unfussy World's End trattoria offers above-average cooking. The best deal is the 2-course lunch – at £8.95, it's the same price as the house wine. You choice might be gnocchi with spinach, bacon and cheese followed by chicken and asparagus in white wine sauce. You would need to stick to salads and pasta to dine à la carte within our budget. / 11.45 pm; closed Sun D.

The Lexington W1 £17* -
Lexington St   0171-434 3401   3–2D
Standards have been erratic of late, but this quirky and Bohemian modern British restaurant is Soho offers an evening menu which is enough of a bargain to be worth chancing – we would not particularly recommend a visit at other times. Your 2-course dinner (£10.95, 6.30pm-9pm) might be tiger prawn and chicken salad with Japanese dressing followed by pan-fried calf's liver with sweet tomatoes, washed down by house wine at £10 a bottle. / 11 pm; closed Sat L & Sun.

Lisboa Patisserie W10 £ 3 ★★
57 Golborne Rd   0181-968 5242   6–1A
Not only top quality snacks at great prices – ham and cheese croissant (£1.20), custard tart (55p), coffee (65p) – but also a street-credible North Kensington location ensures that there's always a trendy crush at this Portuguese pâtisserie. Take the Guardian. / 8 pm; no credit cards; no booking.

The Little Bay NW6 £ 10 Ⓐ
228 Belsize Rd   0171-372 4699   1–2B
This cosy, buzzing Kilburn bistro serves up tasty and filling Mediterranean fare at incredibly low prices – you can easily have a 3-course meal here and stay within budget. Starters, all at £1.85 might include moules marinières, main courses (all £4-£5) could be rump steak or salmon stuffed with vegetable mousse, and puddings such as profiteroles (£1.65) would be typical typical choices from the blackboard menus. Amazingly, prices are even cheaper if you eat before 7pm! House wine at £7.65 a bottle contributes to the party atmosphere. / 11.45 pm; no credit cards.

Little Havana WC2 £19* Ⓐ
Queens House, 1 Leicester Place   0171-287 0101   4–3B
Situated just above the tourist mayhem of Leicester Square, this new Cuban establishment appears to be making above-average efforts, at least by theme joint standards, to provide real food. You would have to choose quite carefully – perhaps Cuban Caviar (£3.95) followed by roast vegetable tortilla (£6.95) – to keep within our price range, though, and you could blow the budget easily with a couple of tequilas in the lofty bar. House wine is a steep £12.95 a bottle.
/ 12.30 pm; closed Sat L.

Lou Pescadou SW5   £15*   ★★
241 Old Brompton Rd   0171-370 1057   5–3A
Sadly, good Gallic cooking, especially with a fish emphasis, is usually out of the price-range of this guide. That makes it all the more worth seeking out the 3-course lunchtime menu (£9.90) at this long-established Earl's Court spot. You might have Chinese prawns, then beef stew, followed by crêpes Suzettes, all washed down by house wine at £10.50 a bottle.
/ Midnight.

Luigi's Delicatessen SW10   £12   ★★
359 Fulham Rd   0171-351 7825   5–3B
It's not much to look at, but this unpretentious, somewhat chaotic Italian diner has a cult following among the younger Chelsea Eurocrowd. Culinarily speaking, the attraction is the very good snacks, such as ciabatta sandwiches, risotti and pastas (all for under a fiver). Dinner-time opening is a recent innovation, when slightly more ambitious (and expensive) dishes are available, but costs are kept low by a BYO policy.
/ 8 pm, Sat 6 pm; closed Sun; no credit cards; no booking.

Lunch EC1   £10   -
60 Exmouth Market   0171-278 2420   9–1A
Those who believe that decoration is a sin will feel very much at home at this uncompromisingly modernistic Clerkenwell deli/café (which benefits from an unusually large garden). You might have a soup with a baguette (£2.20), a Greek salad (£2.25) or coq au vin with mash (£3.95). No alcohol – drink coffee (from £1) or fresh juices (£1.50). / 5.45 pm; L only; closed Sat & Sun; no credit cards; no smoking 12.30–2.30pm; no booking.

Ma Goa SW15   £19   ★★
244 Upper Richmond Rd   0181-780 1767   10–2B
This family-run Goan bistro in Putney has an approach very unlike the general run of London subcontinentals, and offers light and interesting cooking at reasonable prices. You might start with swordfish pakora in beer batter (£4), for example, with a main course of pork vindaloo in Goan liquor, red chilli and garlic (£7.50). The house wine is £8.75 a bottle. / 11 pm; closed Mon, Tue & Sat L, Sun D.

Made in Italy SW3   £14   ★
249 King's Rd   0171-352 1880   5–3C
Erratic, but popular and welcoming pizza-and-pasta stop on the distant-Chelsea strip, where many of the other 'attractions' tend to the dubious Dôme and Café Rouge variety. Here you get real food (most main dishes around the £6 mark) in unpretentious surroundings. The house wine is £9 a bottle. / 11.30 pm; no Amex; to book need 6+.

Madhu's Brilliant UB1   £15   ★
39 South Road   0181-574 1897   1–3A
Young glitzy upstart sibling to the original Brilliant, which has the benefit for curry pilgrims that is is closer to Southall BR (five minutes away up the high street) and has notably friendly service. The 3-course set lunch (£12.50) offers good value, but the à la carte prices are all well within budget, with starters at £4-£6 (say, chilli chicken and deep-fried mixed vegetables), mains (spring lamb in ginger and garlic) around £7 and rice at £2. Drink Indian beers (Cobra, £3.50) or the house wine (£8 a bottle). / 11.30 pm; closed Tue, Sat L & Sun L.

Maison Bertaux W1   £5   A
28 Greek St   0171-437 6007   4–2A
For character on a budget, you won't do much better than the oldest pâtisserie in town (1871), where erratic staff contribute to the charm of these intimate and laid-back Soho premises. Croissants start at 90p, and other pâtisserie items from £1.50, with coffee from £1.20. / 8.30 pm; no credit cards; no smoking area.

Malabar W8   £18   A★
27 Uxbridge St   0171-727 8800   6–2B
A perennial success-story, this civilised subcontinental, just off Notting Hill Gate, offers reliably good cooking at reasonable prices. Top value is the Sunday buffet lunch (£7.50), but even à la carte you should be able to eat here quite comfortably within our price-limit – most curries are around the £7 mark, and the house wine is £8.65 a bottle. / 11.15 pm; no Amex.

Malabar Junction WC1   £19   ★
107 Gt Russell St   0171-580 5230   2–1C
Some restaurants never seem to get the following they deserve, and this smart Bloomsbury Indian, which boasts an impressive rear conservatory, is a classic example. Starters are no more than a fiver, and with mains, such as Malabar chilli chicken (£7), all served with rice and bread, a 2-course meal just fits our budget. The house wine is £10 a bottle. / 11.30 pm; no Switch; no smoking area.

La Mancha SW15   £18   A
32 Putney High St   0181-780 1022   10–2B
Putney is still rather thinly provided with good places to eat, so it's worth knowing about this somewhat cavernous bar. The top budget choice would be to make a meal of tapas (mainly £3.50-£5), or, in the upstairs restaurant you could, with reasonable care, dine within our price limit. The house wine is £9.25 a bottle. / Mon-Thu 11 pm, Fri-Sun 11.30 pm.

Mandalay W2 £11 ★
444 Edgware Rd   0171-258 3696   8–4A
This exceedingly friendly, family-run ethnic café, in converted shop premises just around the corner from Lords, dishes up some interesting and well spiced Burmese cooking (reflecting a mixture of Indian and oriental influences). The lunchtime special, at £5.40, buys you a selection of dishes (and coffee) – at other times, main dishes, such as crispy fried fish in spicy sauce, or noodles with king prawns and coconut, cost about the same. With starters around £3, and house wine at £7.50, you can dine here really well within budget. / 10.30 pm; closed Sun; no smoking.

Mandarin Kitchen W2 £16 ★★
14-16 Queensway   0171-727 9012   6–2C
No-nonsense seafood – served without much in the way of ambience or charm – is what this famous Bayswater Chinese is all about. Steamed scallops (£1.80) and squid in ginger sauce (£7.90) are typical of the sort of dishes which make a visit here special. The house wine is £9.90 a bottle. / 11.30 pm.

Mandeer WC1 £14 -
8 Bloomsbury Way   0171-242 6202   2–1D
One of London's most venerable veggie Indians has, thanks to redevelopment, lost its characterful old basement premises. The new Bloomsbury-fringe setting retain a surprising amount of the old spirit though, and it still dishes up a tasty and inexpensive lunch buffet (£3.90), and rather pricier and more ambitious fare by night. House wine is £8.95 a bottle. / 10 pm; closed Sun; no smoking.

Mandola W11 £15 A★
139 Westbourne Grove   0171-229 4734   6–1B
It's not just the absence of much in the way of competition on the Sudanese front which makes this Notting Hill spot so popular. The candlelit, Bohemian dining room is very atmospheric, and the food is interesting, tasty and well-spiced – talapia fish with a potent chilli sauce (£6.95), for example. BYO (£1 a head corkage) helps keep costs under control.
/ 10.30 pm; no credit cards.

Mango Room NW1 £16 A
10 Kentish Town Rd   0171-482 5065   8–3B
This Camden Town yearling has successfully attracted the fickle local trendies, with its bright décor and imaginative British-Caribbean fusion menu. If, after a starter of, say, salt cod fritters with apple chutney (£3.50), you don't fancy the 'famous' Camden curried goat (£7), you could opt for likes of Creole snapper in mango and green pepper sauce (£7.50). The house wine will set you back £9.50 a bottle. / 11 pm; no Amex.

Manna NW3 £15 ★
4 Erskine Rd   0171-722 8028   8–3B
This venerable Primrose Hill establishment – there's been a veggie restaurant on this site for 31 years – maintains its following. Top value is the 2-course lunch for £5 (choose two courses from soup, salad and pudding). A la carte dishes are the likes of spinach and grilled aubergine lasagne verde (£6.95). The organic house wine is £10.50 a bottle, or non-organic for a couple of pounds less. / 11 pm; D only, except Sun when L & D; no Amex; no smoking.

Manorom WC2 £18 -
16 Maiden Ln   0171-240 4139   4–3D
Located in a small side street, this cosy, intimate and welcoming Thai restaurant makes a quiet retreat from Covent Garden. The food has no great aspirations, but it's not pricey and the place always fills up early. The best value is from the 3-course set meals (lunch £9.95, dinner £12.95). House wine is £9.50 a bottle. / 11 pm; closed Sat L & Sun.

Manzara W11 £11 -
24 Pembridge Rd   0171-727 3062   6–2B
It doesn't have what you might describe as a de luxe setting, but this Turkish café, just off Notting Hill Gate, does offer sustaining, good-value cooking. You might have mixed meze (£4.45) or a kebab with yoghurt and pitta bread (£4.95), washed down with house wine at £7.95 a bottle. Make sure you leave space for a pastry (baklava is 55p). / 11.30 pm; no smoking.

Manzi's WC2 £19* Ⓐ
1 Leicester St   0171-734 0224   4–3A
A visit to this Theatreland fish parlour tells you everything about what it was like to dine out in London half a century ago (and the establishment itself is older than that). It's out of our price range à la carte, but pre-theatre (until 7.30pm) you can have a classic 3-course old-style dinner – perhaps minestrone soup, poached salmon with Hollandaise sauce, then strawberry tart – for £13.50, washed down by house wine at £9.50 a bottle. / 11.30 pm, Cabin Room 10.30 pm; closed Sun L.

Maroush £14 ★
I) 21 Edgware Rd, W2   0171-723 0773   6–1D
II) 38 Beauchamp Pl, SW3   0171-581 5434   5–1C
III) 62 Seymour St, W1   0171-724 5024   2–2A
As you might gather from house wine priced at £17.50 a bottle, even the café sections of these swanky Lebanese restaurants are not what you would describe as cheap. Especially if you're looking for a lively late-night snack, however, do bear them in mind – kebabs and meze are in the £3-£4 range. Meaty main courses start at about £12, and budget diners can drink beer for £3, or fresh juices from around £2.50. / W2 1.30 am, SW3 4.30 am, W1 11.30 pm.

The Marquis W1 £20* 🅐★
121a Mount St   0171-499 1256   3–3B
Frantic at lunchtime and calmer in the evening, this understated Mayfair establishment offers a 2-course set menu for £14.50 (always available). The choices might include goat's cheese and sun-dried tomato salad, roast monkfish wrapped in smoked salmon and banoffi crumble. With house wine at £11.50 a bottle, you will, frankly, probably spend a fraction over our price-limit, but if you want to eat on a budget in the heart of Mayfair, this is just about the only show in town. / 10.45 pm; closed Sat L & Sun; smart casual.

Mas Café W11 £15* 🅐
6-8 All Saints Rd   0171-243 0969   6–1B
It's as a brunch spot that this relaxed North Kensington hang-out is most worth knowing about. On a weekend morning, you can fortify yourself with dishes such as eggs Benedict (£5.50) and spicy chicken burgers (£7), which you can wash down with fresh juices from £2.50. House wine is £9.50 a bottle. / 11.30 pm; D only (also brunch, Sat & Sun); no Amex; no brunch bookings.

The Mason's Arms SW8 £15 🅐★
169 Battersea Park Rd   0171-622 2007   10–1C
It may have an unpromising location (by Battersea Park railway station), but this stripped down gastropub has maintained its appeal as a trendy younger scene for a number of years now (and, indeed, is sometimes too crowded). The menu may seem to strive rather hard to be eclectic – you might have antipasti (£4.90) followed by Cajun chicken with mustard fruit sauce (£8.10) – but the results are often quite satisfying. The house wine is £8.65 a bottle. / 10 pm.

Matsuri SW1 £19* ★
15 Bury St   0171-839 1101   3–3D
This St James's Japanese is mega-pricey by night. At lunchtime, though, you can enjoy the teppan-yaki specials – say, beef teriyaki (£14) or vegetarian (£10) – which, complete with rice, miso soup, pickles and tea, come within our price range. Entertainment comes free, too – your meal is prepared in front of you by the knife-juggling chefs. Drink Kirin beer (£3) or hot sake (from £7 a flask). / 10 pm; closed Sun; no Switch.

Mayflower W1 £16 ★
68-70 Shaftesbury Ave   0171-734 9207   4–3A
Don't let the spooky tinted windows put you off visiting this bright and clean Chinatown spot – the plain interior offers some of the most authentic chow in town. Crispy aromatic duck with all the trimmings (£6.80) followed by chicken in black bean sauce (£5.90) would be a sensible selection – avoid the set menus unless you want to be treated like a stupid tourist. The house wine is £8 a bottle. / 3.45 am; D only.

Mediterranean Café W1 £14 ★
18 Berwick St   0171-437 0560   3–2D
This odd Soho newcomer offers surprisingly good cooking in a setting so worn out that you assume the place must have been there forever. Top value is the 2-course set lunch (£5), but even à la carte you can dine quite inexpensively on dishes such as baked avocado (£3.20) and veal with cheese and asparagus (£7.50). The house wine is £8 a bottle. / Midnight, Fri–Sat 1 am; no Amex.

Mediterraneo W11 £18 𝔸★
37 Kensington Park Rd   0171-792 3131   6–1A
Only a few doors from its trendy sister, Osteria Basilico, this newer and somewhat less rustic venue has already accumulated a similarly strong Notting Hill following. You might start with a rocket salad with tiger prawns and palm hearts (£6), followed by a home-made pasta, say tortelloni with ricotta and spinach (£6.80). The house wine is £9.50 a bottle. / 11.30 pm.

Melati W1 £16 ★
21 Great Windmill St   0171-437 2745   3–2D
Long known as a haven of value near Piccadilly Circus, this cramped Indonesian bistro offers consistently interesting food at reasonable prices. Chicken satay (£5.55), spicy coconut chicken soup (£2.95) and crispy chilli chicken (£5.45) are typical dishes. House wine is £8.45 a bottle. / 11.30 pm, Fri & Sat 12.30 am; no Switch.

Mesclun N16 £18 ★
24 Stoke Newington Ch St   0171-249 5029   1–1C
The culinary reputation of this imaginative Stoke Newington venture is growing, so, as its aspirations creep up, you'll have to choose carefully to eat within our price-limit. You could avoid the pricey starters (all around the £5 mark), and go for mains and puddings, perhaps roast duck with teriyaki sauce (£10.95), then hot chocolate brownie sundae (£3.25). A bottle of the house wine is £9.95. / 11 pm; D only (but open all day Sun); no Amex.

Meson don Felipe SE1 £14   𝔸
53 The Cut   0171-928 3237   9–4A
The consistent quality of the tapas is not the only attraction of this lively Waterloo bar – there's always a lively crowd and often live music. Drink house wine (£9.45) or sangria (large jug, £11.50) with a selection of the tasty dishes, such as garlic prawns, Spanish tortilla and patatas bravas, all priced around £3-£5. / 11 pm; closed Sun; no Amex; book pre 7.30 pm only.

Le Metro SW3 £16 ★
28 Basil St   0171-589 6286   5–1D
If you want a break from shopping at Harrods, this discreet wine bar offers an ideal bolt-hole. Situated in a stylishly understated basement, it offers a limited but well priced menu from which Mediterranean fish soup (£4.95), Caesar salad (£6.75) and risotto with mussels and fennel (£6.95) would be typical selections. There is a large wine list – the patron has his own cuvée – starting at £9.85 a bottle.
/ 10.30 pm; closed Sun; no booking at L.

Mildreds W1 £13 ★
58 Greek St   0171-494 1634   4–2A
There's nothing dainty about the portions of vegetarian food on offer at this Soho café, which perhaps accounts for its continuing popularity – there's usually a crush. The menu is always evolving – you might start with globe artichokes filled with Ricotta and Parmesan (£3.50), and follow with Italian farmhouse pie (£6.20). The house wine is £8.50 a bottle.
/ 11 pm; closed Sun; no credit cards; no smoking; no booking.

Mirabelle W1 £20*   𝔸★★
56 Curzon St   0171-499 4636   3–4B
This one's a cheat – you couldn't, to be honest, quite stay within our budget here. But everyone has to break the rules occasionally, and this place – Marco Pierre White's glamorous pride of Mayfair – is worth it! The 2-course set lunch (£14.95, including coffee) might comprise truffled cabbage soup, followed by roast lamb. The wine list stretches to thousands of pounds a bottle, but kicks off at £16.50.
/ Midnight; no smoking area.

Momo W1 £18* A★
25 Heddon St   0171-434 4040   3–2C
At lunchtime, you probably won't find yourself sitting next to Naomi, Kate, Claudia et al, but you might still come across the occasional beautiful person enjoying the bargain 2-course menu (£12.50, including coffee) at this still mega-trendy West End Moroccan. Your choice might be cod goujons in anchovy butter, followed by a lamb tagine. The house wine is £10.50 a bottle. / 11.15 pm; closed Sat L & Sun.

Mon Plaisir WC2 £12* A★★
21 Monmouth St   0171-836 7243   4–2B
Re-opening in Spring 1999, after a major fire, this delightfully old-fashioned Gallic favourite in Covent Garden will return – we are promised – pretty much unchanged. Presumably, it will still offer one of the best pre-theatre deals in the West End, with the set menu (£11.95) including two courses, service, coffee and a glass of wine. / 11.15 pm; closed Sat L & Sun.

Mona Lisa SW10 £ 9 ★
417 King's Rd   0171-376 5447   5–3B
A Chelsea-fringe location together with some top-value Italian home cooking attracts an odd but interesting mix of people – from toffs to builders – to this World's End greasy spoon. There's a 3-course set menu for £5.50 (always available), but eating à la carte won't set you back very much more. The house wine is £7 a bottle. / 10.45 pm; closed Sun D; no credit cards.

Monsieur Max TW12 £18* ★
133 High St, Hampton Hill   0181-979 5546   1–4A
Budget diners should seize the opportunity of the set lunch menu (two courses, £11) to check out this informal restaurant, whose reputation for top-quality Gallic fare belies its small size and obscure Hampton Hill location. You might have guinea fowl and root vegetable confit followed by salmon with beetroot, washed down by house wine at £9.50 a bottle. / 10.30 pm; closed Sat L; no Amex.

Moshi Moshi Sushi £ 13 ★
Unit 24, Liverpool St Station, EC2   0171-247 3227   9–2D
7-8 Limeburner Ln, EC4   0171-248 1808   9–2A
Conveyor-belt sushi cafés – where you take your dishes off the belt, and pay per plate (90p-£2.50) – may seem a bit of a cliché nowadays, but the originators of the trend still offer good value, and they're extremely popular, especially at lunchtime. Away from the belt, set meals are available from a fiver upwards. The house wine is £8.80 a bottle, or Japanese beer is £2.50 a bottle. / 9 pm; closed Sat & Sun; no Amex or Switch; EC2 no smoking, EC4 no smoking area; no booking.

Moxon's SW4 £18 ★
14 Clapham Park Road   0171-627 2468   10–2D
It may be implausibly located, opposite a big branch of Sainsbury's, but this Clapham newcomer already has a strong reputation thanks to the quality of its mainly fishy cooking. You'll have to take some care to stay within our price limit, but it's perfectly possible it you have, say, Caesar salad with caramelised walnuts (£3.95), with, maybe, pan-fried mackerel with relish (£8.25) to follow. The house wine is £9.95 a bottle.
/ 10.30 pm; closed Mon; no Amex.

Mr Kong WC2 £14 ★
21 Lisle St   0171-437 7341   4–3A
For Cantonese cuisine with a bit of a difference it's worth seeking out this Chinatown spot, where an inspired chef/patron offers a menu with some unusual specials. Don't be put off by the rather grungy basement – delights such as baked frog's legs and deep-fried stuffed beancurd skin (both £7.50) will justify the trip. The house wine is £7.50 a bottle.
/ 2.45 am.

Museum St Café WC1 £16 ★
47 Museum St   0171-405 3211   2–1C
After a spell as a 'proper restaurant', this well-established spot near the British Museum has reverted to a style closer to that which its name suggests – a pleasant place for breakfast, lunch or tea. The fare is now all-vegetarian – you might start with lentil and chestnut soup (£4.25), followed by aubergine and Parmesan tart (£7.50). The house wine is £10 a bottle.
/ L only; no smoking.

Nautilus NW6 £13 ★
27–29 Fortune Gn Rd   0171-435 2532   1–1B
There's a wide range of fish (from £7.50, including chips) to be had at this venerable Kosher chippy in West Hampstead (where all the fish is fried in matzo meal). If you're really hungry, there's plenty of budget left for you to kick off your meal with smoked salmon (£3) or soup (£1.80), washed down by house wine at £8 a bottle, (or, for the full effect, drink retsina, £6). / 10.15 pm; closed Sun; no credit cards; no booking.

Nayab SW6 £18 ★
309 New King's Rd   0171-731 6993   10–1B
Cooking standards are high and prices are moderate at this long-established Parson's Green Indian – it's only real drawback is rather oppressive décor. The menu includes lots of non-standard dishes, few of them priced at more than £7. The house wine is £8.95 a bottle. / Midnight; smart casual.

Neal's Yard Dining Rooms WC2 £10 ★
14 Neal's Yd   0171-379 0298   4–2C
Global veggie fare at reasonable prices makes this Covent Garden café an ideal daytime destination for anyone seeking a quick bite in the centre of town. The menu has a simple formula of light meals – such as falafel and Mexican tortillas – all at £5.85, and more substantial dishes, including Indian thali and Turkish meze, all at £7.85. BYO, or drink fresh juices (from £1.35). / generally 7.30 pm, summer Mon & Sat 5 pm; closed Sun; no credit cards; no smoking; no booking.

New World W1 £13 -
Gerrard Pl   0171-734 0677   4–3A
With its gaudy red and gold façade, this large and chaotic spot is a Chinatown landmark. Culinarily, it's the lunchtime dim sum (served from trolleys at £1.50 per item) which is the prime attraction. Dinner is less exciting, but with a long menu from which you can easily find a selection to stay within budget. House wine is £8.50 a bottle. / 11.45 pm; no booking Sun L.

Newton's SW4 £18* -
33 Abbeville Rd   0181-673 0977   10–2D
They offer nothing too demanding on the culinary front, but these modern British local bistros in Clapham and Fulham provide a competent overall package. A la carte, you would probably spend somewhat outside our price limit, but there are both 2-course set lunch (£5) and dinner (£12.95) menus which will keep you comfortably within it. The latter might comprise smoked chicken and orange salad followed by fish skewers with Hollandaise sauce. House wine is £9.50 a bottle. / 11.30 pm; no smoking area.

Nine Golden Square W1 £18* ★★
9 Golden Sq   0171-439 2424   3–2D
Golden Square may only be a couple of hundred yards from Piccadilly Circus, but somehow it's so far off all the beaten tracks that it's often overlooked. In the evening (till 7pm), this modern British restaurant offers great value to get the punters in – for £12.50 you get to make a 2-course selection from the à la carte menu, which might be seared foie gras, followed by grilled fish steak with tomato chutney. The house wine is £9.75 a bottle. / Mon–Wed 10.30 pm, Thu–Sat 11.30 pm; closed Sat L & Sun.

Noho W1 £16 ★
32 Charlotte St   0171-636 4445   2–1C
Staff wearing Thunderbirds-style jackets contribute to the 'jet-age' atmosphere of this slick Fitzrovia noodle-bar, where above-average dishes come at quite reasonable prices. Vegetable rice-paper rolls (£3.75) followed by seafood soba (£7.50) would be a typical selection, with house wine at £8.75 a bottle. / 11.30 pm.

Nontas NW1 £14 ★
14 Camden High St   0171-387 4579   8–3C
A resident cat adds a suitably domestic ambience to this long-established family-run Greek restaurant in Camden Town. For top value, choose the 16-dish meze (£9.95), washed down with house wine at an ultra-modest £8.60 a litre.
/ 11.30 pm; closed Sun; no Switch.

Noor Jahan SW5 £18 ★
2a Bina Gdns   0171-373 6522   5–2B
In a quietly residential part of South Kensington, this long-established Indian maintains a loyal following thanks to the reasonable prices of its consistently good-quality curry house fare (if not to its rather unwelcoming service). Most standard main dishes are around the £8 mark, and the house wine is £9.95 a bottle. / 11.30 pm; no Switch.

The North Pole SE10 £19* ★
131 Greenwich High Road   0181-853 3020   1–3D
Unless you go for the £12.50 set lunch, you'll have to choose quite carefully to stay within our price-bracket in the first-floor dining room of this trendy Greenwich pub-conversion. If you should find yourself heading towards the meridian, however – which, as the You Know What approaches, you quite possibly will – this is one of the few places of any note thereabouts. A relatively economical meal might be soup (£3.80), followed by pappardelle in fava bean and tomato sauce (£9.50). The house wine is £9.50 a bottle. / 10.15 pm; closed Mon.

Noto £10 ★
2-3 Bassishaw Highwalk, EC2   0171-256 9433   9–3B
7 Bread St, EC4   0171-329 8056   9–2C
Fast food, Japanese-style, is the proposition at these very popular City noodle parlours. A set meal of chicken teriyaki with rice and soup will set you back £6, and there is house wine at £10 a bottle, or Japanese beers from £2.80. / EC2 10.15 pm - EC4 8.45 pm, Sat 6 pm; EC2 closed Sat & Sun – EC4 closed Sat D & Sun; EC2 no Amex – EC4 no credit cards; EC2 no smoking at L; EC2 no booking for L - EC4 no bookings.

Odette's NW1 £17* A★★
130 Regent's Pk Rd   0171-586 5486   8–3B
Primrose Hill is one of the most characterful parts of London, and this is its prettiest restaurant. Decorated with hundreds of mirrors, it makes a great place for a special treat. Astonishingly, they do a 3-course lunch for £10 – you might have onion and potato soup, roast duck and then quince tart. Even the house wine, at £10.95 a bottle, is hardly overpriced. Unsurprisingly, evening prices are well outside our budget.
/ 11 pm; closed Sat L & Sun.

The Old School Thai SW11 £15 ★
147 Lavender Hl   0171-228 2345   10–1C
This Battersea Thai extends a warm welcome, and the cooking, if fairly standard, is good, too. You might have mixed starters (£9.60 for two), followed by red duck curry with pineapple and bamboo shoots (£4.95). The house wine is £9 a bottle. / 11 pm; closed Sun L; no smoking area; bookings only after 5pm.

Oliveto SW1 £19* ★
49 Elizabeth St   0171-730 0074   2–4A
Belgravia is about as close to Hell as London gets for budget diners, so it's worth knowing about this modishly smart, if not particularly inexpensive, Italian. To keep within our limit, you would have to stick to pizza – no great hardship as it's the best thing on the menu – or pasta (both around £8) and a pudding (£4.50). The house wine is £10 a bottle. / 11.30 pm.

Oriental City Food Court NW9 £10 ★
399 Edgware Rd   0181-200 0009   1–1A
The food court of this extraordinary Japanese shopping mall (whose original owners, Yaohan, sold up last year) brings the flavours of the exotic East to not-so-exotic Colindale. It's not an especially comfortable experience, but you do get the opportunity to try a bewildering range of oriental dishes and you're unlikely to spend much more than a tenner. / 11 pm; no Amex.

Osteria Antica Bologna SW11 £18 ★
23 Northcote Rd   0171-978 4771   10–2C
For a taste of rustic Italy, you won't find a much better combination of setting and food than this long-established Battersea 'rosticceria'. For ultimate value, visit at lunchtime (Mon-Sat), for the 2-course set menu (£7.50), when you might have vegetable soup, followed by trout with mint, tomato and Mozzarella. A la carte, there are pastas (£5-£7) or, at slightly higher prices, meat dishes, many using organic ingredients. A carafe of house wine is £7.90. / 11 pm, Fri & Sat 11.30 pm.

Osteria Basilico W11   £19*   A★
29 Kensington Pk Rd   0171-727 9957   6–1A
The 'Tuscan farmhouse' setting is just part of the appeal which ensures that this Notting Hill spot is perennially packed with trendy local urbanites. To keep within our budget, you would have to choose carefully, but it's possible if you had something like deep-fried squid and prawns (£4.90) followed by chicken Milanese (£7.90). A carafe of house wine is £8.
/ 11 pm; no booking Sat L.

Palatino W4   £18   ★
6 Turnham Green Ter   0181-994 0086   7–2A
From the outside, you might think that this was just a standard local Italian, but the food's more-than-averagely interesting, and just occasionally hits the heights. You'll have to stick to the cheaper items to stay within our price range, perhaps marinated grilled vegetables (£3.95), followed by spaghetti with sausage, leeks and Dolcelatte (£6.95), washed down with house wine at £10.25 a bottle. / 11 pm; no smoking area.

The Papaya Tree W8   £14   -
209 Kensington High St   0171-937 2260   7–1D
With starters such as delicate steamed dumplings with minced pork and prawns at £3.95 and red chicken curry at a mere £5.50, it's possible to accommodate a visit to this family-run Kensington basement Thai within our budget at any time. For a real bargain, however, go at lunchtime and have a one-plate meal for a fiver. The house wine is £9.95 a bottle. / 11 pm; closed Sun; no smoking area.

Pasha SW7   £18*   A★
1 Gloucester Rd   0171-589 7969   5–1B
House wine at £11.50 a bottle is a fair indication that, à la carte at least, this trendy South Kensington Moroccan is out of our price range, but if you stick to the set lunch (2-courses £11.95, 3-courses £13.95) your choice might include couscous salad with char-grilled vegetables, and lamb tagine. Culinary achievements may not be high, but for sheer glamour on a limited budget, this is a steal. / 11.30 pm; closed Sun.

Pasha N1   £15   ★
301 Upper St   0171-226 1454   8–3D
Ever popular with the locals, this Islington Turk offers basic fare at decent prices. You could eat here at any time within our price range, but lunchtime visitors find the best deals – a 2-course meal for £5.50, or go for broke with the Pasha lunch, which comprises eight cold, and five hot meze for £9.95 (minimum of two). A bottle of house wine is £8.95.
/ 11.30 pm, Fri & Sat midnight; no Switch.

Patio W12 £14 🅐
5 Goldhawk Rd   0181-743 5194   7–1C
How, especially given its prominent Shepherd's Bush corner site, can we have for so long overlooked this Polish gem? No matter – it's worth a trip, especially for a party night out, for its fun atmosphere and the top-value 3-course menu (always available, £9.90). That might comprise dumplings, Polish-style lamb and home-made puddings such as baked cheesecake. The menu includes a free shot of vodka, but if more provisions are necessary, house wine is £8 a bottle. / Midnight; closed Sat L & Sun L; no smoking area.

Pâtisserie Valerie £10 🅐★
105 Marylebone High St, W1   0171-935 6240   2–1A
44 Old Compton St, W1   0171-437 3466   4–2A
RIBA Centre, 66 Portland Pl, W1   0171-631 0467   2–1B
8 Russell St, WC2   0171-240 0064   4–3D
215 Brompton Rd, SW3   0171-823 9971   5–2C
The array of tempting goodies in the window make this impressive chain of pâtisseries hard to resist. They are not just for the sweet-of-tooth, though – there's plenty in the savoury line, such as toasted sandwiches (£3), small salads (£2.50), mini quiches (£4.50) and so on. The menu and style varies somewhat from branch to branch – our favourites are the Soho original (for the definitive croissant) and the big and bustly outlet near Harrods. / 6 pm-8 pm, Sun earlier; Portland Pl, closed Sun; no smoking area; no booking.

Paulo's W6 £16 🅐★
30 Greyhound Rd   0171-385 9264   7–2C
If you're looking for a party venue (especially one with a high veggie content), you could do much worse than this jovial Brazilian establishment, which Paulo and Gillian run in the front room of their Hammersmith home. For £10.50 (less on Sun L or Tue D), you help yourself from buffet – eat as much as you like from the selection of ten hot dishes (for example, fish with coconut and peanuts) and ten salads. A traditional Brazilian pudding, quindim (made with coconut and cream) will set you back £2.65, and house wine is £8.85 a bottle. / 10.30 pm; D only – Sun L only, closed Mon; no credit cards.

The Pepper Tree SW4 £13 ★
19 Clapham Common S'side   0171-622 1758   10–2D
This Thai refectory in Clapham is one of the most genuinely popular places to eat in south London, and you'll probably find that you have to queue. Good prices for quality dishes is part of the attraction – barbecued prawns (£2.95) and green chicken curry (£3.75), for example – and the house wine is £7.95 a bottle. / 11 pm, Mon and Sun 10.30 pm; no Amex; no smoking area; no D bookings.

La Perla WC2 £16 -
28 Maiden Ln   0171-240 7400   4–4D
Under the same ownership as the well-known Café Pacifico, this Covent Garden cantina is becoming at least as popular as its parent. The bar is where the fun is – both there and the restaurant offer Mexican dishes that will not break the bank. Appetisers include nachos with cheese and jalapeños (£2.95), with, perhaps, chuletas de cordero to follow (lamb cutlets with sweet potato mash, £8.25). The house wine is £9.50 a bottle, or a bottle of Dos Equis will set you back £2.35. / 11 pm; closed Sun D.

Le P'tit Normand SW18 £15* ★★
185 Merton Rd   0181-871 0233   10–2B
Lunches (especially Mon-Fri) are the top-value choice at this quirky, unpretentious family-run restaurant in Southfields, when for a fiver you can enjoy a menu offering onion soup followed by salmon steak with chives. You could – with care – dine here within our price-bracket, and on Sundays there's a 3-course lunch for £11.95. The house wine is £8.95 a bottle. / 10 pm, Fri & Sat 11 pm; closed Sat L.

Phoenix Bar & Grill SW15 £16* ★
Pentlow St   0181-780 3131   10–1A
Bright and airy – stark, some might say – Putney spot, where, to keep comfortably within our price-limit, you will have to stick to the 2-course set lunch and early-evening menu (£12, Sun-Thu, until 7.45pm). Even so, there are some interesting choices to be had – you might choose seared gravadlax with orange Hollandaise, followed by chicken livers and roast Jerusalem artichokes. House wine is £9.50 a bottle. / 11.30 pm, Sun 10 pm; closed Sat L.

Phuket SW11 £15 ★
246 Battersea Pk Rd   0171-223 5924   10–1C
This Battersea Thai is a pretty standard sort of place, but is worth knowing about in that rather thinly provided area. The set dinner (£12.50), comprises mixed starters, sweet and sour pork, egg fried rice, pudding and coffee – or you can go à la carte for not very much more. House wine is just £6.95 a bottle. / 11.30 pm; D only.

La Piragua N1   £14   🄰★
176 Upper St   0171-354 2843   8–2D
The Latin American vibe at this small, lively Islingtonian is not the only draw for the crowd which packs it out nightly – the food, with Colombian specialites, is both interesting and good value. Starters, mostly priced at £1.95, include empanadas (deep-fried spicy beef pasties), while main courses range from chilli con carne (£5.95) to excellent steaks (£7.50–£10), served with salad & chips. The all South American wine list starts at £9. / Midnight; no credit cards.

Pizza Metro SW11   £17   ★★
64 Battersea Rise   0171-228 3812   10–2C
Judging from the clientèle, you pretty quickly form the view that this cramped and unpretentious Battersea spot must be an authentic Neapolitan pizzeria, a feeling reinforced by the fact that the pizza from the wood-burning oven is sold by the metre (one metre, at £27, feeds half a dozen people). Alternatively, the seafood dishes, are another 'specialita della casa'. The house wine is £7.95 a bottle. (NB: unusually for a pizzeria, you really must book ahead if you want to dine here.) / 11 pm; closed Mon; D only, Tue-Fri; no Amex.

Pizza On The Park SW1   £14   🄰
11 Knightsbridge   0171-235 5273   2–3A
This airier and grander-than-usual PizzaExpress offers all the usual pizzas (£7) as well as more substantial dishes such as cannelloni (£7.25) and chilli con carne (£6.50). It makes quite an elegant place to kick the day off – they do quite a wide-ranging breakfast menu – and there's also a major cabaret venue in the basement (significant charge). The house wine is £9.75 a bottle. / Midnight; no smoking area; no booking.

Pizza Pomodoro SW3   £16   🄰
51 Beauchamp Pl   0171-589 1278   5–1C
This seedily located Knightsbridge pizzeria, long famed as one of the most reliable late-night venues in town, is always buzzing, thanks to the sheer crush of people and the attraction of a live band nightly. It may be in a basement, but prices are no great bargain – garlic bread to start would set you back £3.45, pizzas are around the £7 mark, and the house wine is £10 a bottle. / 1 am; no booking.

PizzaExpress £12 ★

154 Victoria St, SW1   0171-828 1477   2–4B
10 Dean St, W1   0171-437 9595   3–1D
133 Baker St, W1   0171-486 0888   2–1A
20 Greek St, W1   0171-734 7430   4–2A
21-22 Barrett St, W1   0171-629 1001   3–1A
23 Bruton Pl, W1   0171-495 1411   3–2B
29 Wardour St, W1   0171-437 7215   4–3A
6 Upper St James Street, W1   0171-437 4550   3–2D
7-9 Charlotte St, W1   0171-580 1110   2–1C
30 Coptic St, WC1   0171-636 3232   2–1C
80-81 St Martins Lane, WC2   0171-836 8001   4–3B
9-12 Bow St, WC2   0171-240 3443   4–2D
363 Fulham Rd, SW10   0171-352 5300   5–3B
6-7 Beauchamp Pl, SW3   0171-589 2355   5–1C
Pheasantry, 150-152 King's Road, SW3   0171-351 5031   5–3C
895 Fulham Rd, SW6   0171-731 3117   10–1B
137 Notting Hl Gt, W11   0171-229 6000   6–2B
7 Rockley Rd, W14   0181-749 8582   7–1C
26 Porchester Rd, W2   0171-229 7784   6–1C
252 Chiswick High Rd, W4   0181-747 0193   7–2A
35 Earl's Ct Rd, W8   0171-937 0761   5–1A
335 Upper St, N1   0171-226 9542   8–3D
30 Highgate High Street, N6   0181-341 3434   8–1B
187 Kentish Town Road, NW1   0171-267 0101   8–2B
85-87 Parkway, NW1   0171-267 2600   8–3B
194 Haverstock Hill, NW3   0171-794 6777   8–2A
70 Heath St, NW3   0171-433 1600   8–1A
39-39a Abbey Rd, NW8   0171-624 5577   8–3A
Cardomom Bldg, Shad Thames, SE1   0171-403 8484   9–4D
Chapter Ho, Montague Cl, SE1   0171-378 6446   9–3C
230 Lavender Hill, SW11   0171-223 5677   10–2C
46 Battersea Br Rd, SW11   0171-924 2774   5–4C
305 Up Richmond Rd W, SW14   0181-878 6833   10–2A
144 Up Richmond Rd, SW15   0181-789 1948   10–2B
539 Old York Rd, SW18   0181-877 9812   10–2B
43 Abbeville Rd, SW4   0181-673 8878   10–2D
125 London Wall, EC2   0171-600 8880   9–2B
7-9 St Brides Street, EC4   0171-583 5126   9–2A

Doing one thing, and doing it well, has stood PizzaExpress in good stead for more than 30 years, and its pizzas (£4.50-£7) remain the most reliable pan-metropolitan source of budget sustenance. Some can't help wondering, however, whether – in the group's continuing dash for growth – standards are quite being maintained, and some of the newer branches seem to us to lack soul. The house wine, at £9.65 a bottle, is quite pricey, too. / 11 pm-Midnight - Greek St Wed-Sat 1 am - Chapter Hs 4.30 pm - St Bride's St 10 pm - London Wall Sat & Sun 8 pm; Chapter Hs, St Bride's St, Upper James Street & Bruton Pl closed Sat & Sun (Chapter Hs open Sat in summer); not all branches take bookings.

Pizzeria Castello SE1 £14   A★
20 Walworth Rd   0171-703 2556   1–3C
It may not have the most inviting location – just off the Elephant & Castle roundabout – but this popular pizzeria has long thrived by offering good value for money. The menu offers reliable pizzas and pastas (£4-£6), but also quite a lot besides, with starters such as mixed antipasti (£3.50), and main courses including steak with pepper sauce (£7.95). The house wine is £8.30 a bottle. / 11 pm; closed Sat L & Sun; smart casual.

Pizzeria Condotti W1 £15   A★
4 Mill St   0171-499 1308   3–2C
It's closely related to the PizzaExpress group, but this Mayfair pizzeria has that dash of extra chic you'd hope for, a short step from Savile Row. Especially in the evenings, it's a useful rendezvous for a calm, light meal in civilised surroundings. On the culinary front, it offers some salads and pasta dishes, as well as the usual pizzas (all around the £6-£7 mark), with house wine at £8.95 a bottle. / Midnight; closed Sun.

Pizzeria Franco SW9 £13   ★★
Brixton Market   0171-738 3021   10–2D
Though it's been re-branded by owners, Eco (the Clapham pizzeria), this cramped and popular Brixton market stalwart appears to have changed very little – the sublime pizzas are still reasonably priced (£4.50-£7), you can still BYO (no corkage), and there is still a queue of hungry punters waiting to pounce on your table as you leave. / 5 pm; L only; closed Wed & Sun; no booking.

The Place Below EC2 £12   ★
St Mary-le-Bow, Cheapside   0171-329 0789   9–2C
The City is hardly awash with budget quality dining possibilities, so this well established vegetarian, intriguingly located in the crypt of the impressive St Mary-le-Bow, gets pretty crowded at lunchtimes. The fare is quite innovative, but priced for the affluent local market – a quiche, perhaps mushroom, Stilton and chive, will set you back about £6, or you'll pay a few pence more for something hot, such as ratatouille with tahini mash. Unlicensed – juices and coffee are around the £1.50 mark. / L only; closed Sat & Sun; no Amex; no smoking; no booking.

The Polish Club SW7   £15   Ⓐ
55 Prince's Gt, Exhibition Rd   0171-589 4635   5–1C
A grand, old-fashioned club dining room in South Kensington, which, though run and mainly frequented by Poles, makes outsiders very welcome. A simple 3-course menu (£7.50) is available all day – sitting on the terrace on a sunny day, you might perhaps have cooling cucumber soup, followed by lamb cutlets and then fresh kiwi fruit. For the colder seasons, there are more hearty dishes on offer. The house wine is £9.30 a bottle. / 11 pm; smart casual.

Pollo W1   £ 9   ★
20 Old Compton St   0171-734 5917   4–2A
Steaming bowls of pasta for under a fiver are the attraction which ensures that there's always a crush at this student Soho institution. Other attractions include garlic bread (£1.50), salads (£1.60) and house wine at £5.95 a bottle.
/ Midnight; no credit cards; no booking.

Polygon Bar & Grill SW4   £15*   ★
4 The Polygon, Clapham Old Town   0171-622 1199   10–2D
This modern British brasserie/grill seems rather too stylish for Clapham. A la carte, it's out of our price-range, but in the evenings until 7pm, there's a 2-course menu for £10 – you might have Thai fishcakes followed by Cajun rib-eye steak, washed down with house wine at £9.50 a bottle. / 11.30 pm;
D only Mon-Thu.

Le Pont de la Tour Bar & Grill SE1   £17*   Ⓐ★
36d Shad Thames   0171-403 8403   9–4D
Don't be put off by the fact that the neighbouring restaurant is best known for welcoming prime ministers and presidents – the bar offers a good-value set menu at lunch, and 6pm-7pm. For £10, your choice might be grilled salmon followed by almond tart with blueberry ice-cream, washed down with house wine at £11.90 a bottle. / 11.30 pm; no booking.

Poons WC2   £13   ★
4 Leicester St   0171-437 1528   4–3A
It's dependable, consistent and conveniently located (just north of Leicester Square), so there's always a good flow of regulars at this inexpensive and (moderately) stylish Chinese establishment. Varied set meals are available – for £14, two people can share soup, three main dishes and rice, and even the à la carte menu is not much more expensive. House wine is £7.30 a bottle. / 11.30 pm.

Poons, Lisle Street WC2　　　　　　£13　　★
27 Lisle St　0171-437 4549　4–3B
You eat amongst the clatter and bang of dishes and cutlery at this small and noisy Chinatown café, which combines some of the lowest prices in the West End with generous portions. Top value is the £10 all-day set meal which offers a plethora of choice – soup, fish, mixed barbecue, beef in oyster sauce, chicken and green peppers in black bean sauce… and so it goes on. House wine is £7.30 a bottle. / 11.30 pm; no Amex; no smoking area.

Popeseye W14　　　　　　£18　　★★
108 Blythe Rd　0171-610 4578　7–1C
This Brook Green café is not only one of the least expensive quality steakhouses in London, but also one of the very best. Well-hung Scottish steaks (with chips) come at very reasonable prices – a 6oz sirloin is £9.95. A salad to go with it will set you back £2.95, and the house Rioja is £10.95 a bottle. The new Putney branch offers a very similar formula (277 Upper Richmond Rd, SW15 tel 0181-788 7733). / 10.30 pm; D only; no credit cards.

La Porchetta Pizzeria N4　　　　　　£12　　🅐★
147 Stroud Green Rd　0171-281 2892　8–1D
You won't find much better value than the straightforward fare at this large Finsbury Park pizzeria, nor a livelier atmosphere. With starters, such as stuffed mushrooms, under the £3 mark, most pizzas around a fiver and house wine at only £7.50 a litre, it's no surprise that it's phenomenally popular. / Midnight; closed Sat D & Sun D.

La Poule au Pot SW1　　　　　　£19*　　🅐★★
231 Ebury St　0171-730 7763　5–2D
Consistently voted the most romantic place to dine in London in our annual survey, this old-time, bricks-and-candles Gallic restaurant in Pimlico really is rather special. Unfortunately, evening assignations fall well outside our price-bracket, but there is an excellent 3-course lunch (£13.95, available every day) which is well worth seeking out. The house wine, dispensed in generous bottles from which you pay for what you consume, is £12 per bottle. / 11.15 pm.

Pret A Manger £ 7 ★
12 Kingsgate Pd, Victoria St, SW1   0171-828 1559   2–4B
75b Victoria St, SW1   0171-222 1020   2–4C
120 Baker St, W1   0171-486 2264   2–1A
163 Piccadilly, W1   0171-629 5044   3–3C
173 Wardour St, W1   0171-434 0373   3–1D
18 Hanover St, W1   0171-491 7701   3–2C
298 Regents St, W1   0171-637 3836   4–1A
54-56 Oxford St, W1   0171-636 5750   3–1C
63 Tottenham Court Rd, W1   0171-636 6904   2–1C
7 Marylebone High St, W1   0171-935 0474   2–1A
122 High Holborn, WC1   0171-430 2090   2–1D
240-241 High Holborn, WC1   0171-404 2055   2–1D
77-78 St Martins Ln, WC2   0171-379 5335   4–3B
80 King's Rd, SW3   0171-225 0770   5–2D
8-10 King St, W6   0181-563 1985   7–2C
Kensington Arcade, W8   0171-938 1110   5–1A
27 Islington High St, N1   0171-713 1371   8–3D
157 Camden High St, NW1   0171-284 2240   8–3B
10 Leather Ln, EC1   0171-831 7219   9–2A
140 Bishopsgate, EC2   0171-377 9595   9–2D
17 Eldon St, EC2   0171-628 9011   9–2C
28 Fleet St, EC4   0171-353 2332   9–2A
You seem to see a Pret on every street corner nowadays, but you have to credit these designer-metallic sandwich bars for maintaining their quality through a period of such expansion. Sandwiches (from a selection which changes only slowly) are the main attraction, but there are also salads and sushi selections (£2.70-£4.95), gooey cakes (from £1.10) and coffee at 99p. Add 17.5% VAT to prices given if you're eating in. / 3.30 pm-11 pm; closed Sun except some more central branches; no credit cards; no smoking area; no booking.

The Prince Bonaparte W2 £ 18 ★
80 Chepstow Rd   0171-229 5912   6–1B
What was once a very grotty Bayswater boozer has attracted a large and devoted younger following thanks to the satisfying quality of its modern British grub. You might have the soup of the day (£3.75), followed by roast duck with shallots and spinach for £9 – the same price as a bottle of the house plonk. / 10.20 pm; closed Tue L; no credit cards; no booking.

Pucci Pizza SW3 £ 15 𝔸★
205 King's Rd   0171-352 2134   5–3C
This buzzing Chelsea pizzeria has been HQ to beautiful, young Chelsea for the past 20 years now. It may have no great gastronomic pretensions, but the pizzas, pastas and salads (all around the £6 mark) are all perfectly well done. The house wine is £8.50 a bottle. / 12.30 am; closed Sun; no credit cards.

Purple Sage W1 £18* A★
90-92 Wigmore St   0171-486 1912   3–1A
With its light, air, space and bustle, this upmarket pizzeria has a feeling of downtown Manhattan about it. To stay within our budget, you will have to stick to the house speciality – wood-burning oven pizzas (around £8) – but there are also good meat and fish dishes for a few pounds more. House wine is £9.50 a bottle. / 10.30 pm; closed Sun.

Ragam W1 £12 ★
57 Cleveland St   0171-636 9098   2–1B
This Fitzrovia south Indian vegetarian is neither smart nor spacious, but, for many years, it has secured a following by offering good quality cooking at reasonable prices. There aren't many dishes over £4, so you really can splurge and stay safely within our budget. The house wine is surprisingly expensive at £9.90 a bottle. / 11.30 pm; no Switch.

Randall & Aubin W1 £17* A
16 Brewer St   0171-287 4447   3–2D
Don't let the fact that this very central Soho rôtisserie-cum-seafood bar is housed in a converted delicatessen mislead you into believing that it's cheap – the house wine, for example, is a hefty £11.90 a bottle. If you want to sample a de luxe version of la vie bohème, though, it's quite an amusing place, as long as you accept that some care will be needed to stay within our budget – soup (£2.85) followed by half a dozen oysters (£7) would fit the bill, or stick to the baguettes and salads (£3-£4). / 11 pm.

Rani N3 £15 -
7 Long Ln   0181-349 4386   1–1B
The appeal of this Finchley vegetarian Indian has always been held back by some rather high prices – house wine is £9.70 a bottle, for example – but it undoubtedly offers some interesting and fresh-tasting dishes. The best-value option is the £5.95 set lunch, while in the evening starters are £2.60, and main dishes – perhaps spicy stuffed aubergine – are just south of a fiver. (There used to be a Richmond branch, which is no more.) / 10.30 pm; D only; no smoking area.

Ranoush W2 £12 ★★
43 Edgware Rd   0171-723 5929   6–1D
There are plenty of things you can't do at this late-night Lebanese diner in Bayswater – there's no alcohol, and don't think of paying by cheque or credit card. If in the early hours, however, you're searching for a fresh mango and melon juice (£1.50), a snack such as houmous (£3.50) or a plate of lamb, salad and pitta bread (£9), there is no better place to be.
/ 3 am; no credit cards or cheques.

Ransome's Dock SW11   £19*   A★★
35 Parkgate Rd   0171-223 1611   5–4C
Some of the best modern British cooking (just) south of the river is to be had at this bright and welcoming Battersea restaurant. A la carte, it's out of our budget, but at lunch there's a 2-course menu for £11.50, from which your choice might be carrot and ginger soup followed by smoked haddock fishcakes. The wine list is not cheap – prices start at £13.50 – but is one of the capital's most interesting. / 11 pm; closed Sun D; smart casual.

Raoul's Café W9   £17   ★
13 Clifton Rd   0171-289 7313   8–4A
When it's sunny, the pavement outside this informal bistro/pâtisserie is thronged all day long with locals – young and old alike. You can pop in for a croissant and a cup of coffee, or for something more substantial such as the soup of the day (£3.95) followed by a Mediterranean stew (£7.50). The house wine is £9.50 a bottle. / 10.30 pm; no Amex; no smoking area; book eve only.

Rasa   £18   ★★
6 Dering Street, W1   0171-629 1346   3–2B
55 Stoke Newington Ch St, N16   0171-249 0344   1–1C
The original branch of this south Indian vegetarian (in Stoke Newington) was so successful that a smarter offshoot recently opened in Mayfair, and a further sibling specialising in fish has appeared in Fitzrovia (5 Charlotte Street W1, tel 0171-637 0222). You still get the best value by making the pilgrimage north (and also by going à la carte rather than choosing one of the set menus). Most main dishes are somewhere around a fiver, and house wine is £9.50 a bottle. / 11 pm; closed Sun-Thu L; no smoking.

Rebato's SW8   £19   A
169 South Lambeth Rd   0171-735 6388   10–1D
The outside is pretty grim, but inside you will find few places in town as festive as this Vauxhall Spaniard. The highlight is the tapas bar at the front, which sells tasty and very affordable dishes – for example oyster mushrooms with roasted peppers and prawns, £3.75. To the rear, the restaurant isn't quite such good value, but has its own tacky charm nonetheless. House wine is £8.50 a bottle. / 10.30 pm; closed Sat L & Sun.

The Red Pepper W9 £18 ★
8 Formosa St   0171-266 2708   8–4A
From a base in an inauspicious Maida Vale back street, this bare and somewhat uncompromising pizzeria has established a big reputation. It's all thanks to the quality of the pizzas from the wood-burning oven (around £7.50), and other dishes such as linguine with king prawns (£8). The house wine is £9 a bottle. / 10.45 pm; no Amex.

Reynier Wine Library EC3 £14 𝔸
43 Trinity Sq   0171-481 0415   9–3D
Oenologist's heaven – it's the huge self-selection of bottles, from £6-£200, which is the special delight of a visit to these ancient cellars near Tower Bridge. For £2 corkage, you can then consume your choice in the neighbouring cellar (book ahead), where there's a picnic-like buffet of pâtés, cheeses and salads (£9.95 a head). / L only; closed Sat & Sun.

Riccardo's SW3 £18 ★
126 Fulham Rd   0171-370 6656   5–3B
This Italian tapas restaurant, in pricey Chelsea, makes a popular choice with locals and visitors alike. Everything on the menu here comes in starter-size portions, and most dishes cost under a fiver. Choose between a selection of salads, such as roasted spinach with Parma ham, pasta dishes and pizzas. The house wine is £9.95 a bottle. / Midnight.

Ristorante Italiano W1 £19* 𝔸
54 Curzon St   0171-629 2742   3–3B
Situated in the heart of Mayfair this unfussy, welcoming, comfortable and old-fashioned trattoria is a useful spot for lunch or a light dinner. You will have to choose with some care to remain within our budget – perhaps insalata tricolore (£5) to start followed by chicken and mushroom casserole (£8.50), washed down by house wine at £10 a bottle. / 11.15 pm; closed Sat L & Sun; no smoking area.

RK Stanleys W1 £18 𝔸
6 Little Portland St   0171-462 0099   3–1C
There's no reason, of course, why budget dining can't be trendy too, as is amply demonstrated by this retro-chic 50s-look diner, just north of Oxford Street. Sausages are the speciality, usually quite competently done, with some rather exotic stuffings – Caribbean jerk sausage, for example, which comes with sweet potato mash (£7.95). The drinks list is extensive, with a bewildering range of beers, bottled and draught, a lengthy list of cocktails, and house wine at £10.50 a bottle. / 11.30 pm; closed Sun; no smoking area.

Roussillon SW1 £20* ★★
16 St Barnabas St   0171-730 5550   5–2D
Obscurely located, but ambitious, this restrained Pimlico site benefits from the attentions of a chef who trained with France's only six Michelin star chef, Alain Ducasse. As you might expect, it's out of price range in the evening, but at lunch, for £13.50, you can enjoy two courses, such as beetroot soup followed by roast salmon and mushrooms. House wine is £15 a bottle. / 10.30 pm; ; closed Sun; no Amex.

Royal China £18 ★★
40 Baker St, W1   0171-487 4688   2–1A
13 Queensway, W2   0171-221 2535   6–2C
The Royal Chinas may look like '70s discos, but they're the benchmark of quality for the capital's Chinese restaurants. You can just about keep within our budget at any time, but great-value dim sum (£2 a dish during the day) are the special attraction. A la carte dishes kick off at about £6, and the house wine is £9.50 a bottle. / 11 pm, 11.30 pm Fri & Sat.

La Rueda SW4 £17 𝔸
66-68 Clapham High St   0171-627 2173   10–2D
There is a restaurant (on the fringe of our budget) at this famous, bottle-lined Clapham tapas bar. Give it a miss – the point of this place is the bar and its vibrant atmosphere, especially at weekends, when there's a real buzz, sustained by house wine at £8.50 a bottle. For sustenance, there are all the usual tapas dishes (mostly £3-£5). / 11 pm; book only in restaurant.

Rupee Room EC2 £19 -
10 Copthall Ave   0171-628 1555   9–2C
Anywhere you can eat in the City at less than ruinous cost has something going for it, so it's worth noting the existence of this garishly decorated basement Indian near London Wall. It's no special bargain, though – curries are generally around £9, and the house wine is £7.95 a bottle. / 10 pm; closed Sat & Sun; no smoking area.

S&P £19* ★
181 Fulham Rd, SW3   0171-351 5692   5–2C
9 Beauchamp Pl, SW3   0171-581 8820   5–1C
To keep within budget at these Thai siblings, you will have to watch your pennies – not terribly surprising given that they are to be found in Knightsbridge's trendiest street and on a fashionable Chelsea corner. Even at dinner, prices are not too punishing, but for the best value visit at lunchtime, when there are set menus from £8.95. The house wine is £12 a bottle. / 10.30 pm; no smoking areas.

Sabai Sabai W6 £19 ★
270-272 King St   0181-748 7363   7–2B
It may be something of an atmosphere-free zone, but nevertheless this airy Hammersmith Thai has a steady following thanks to the quality of its cooking. Starters, such as spring rolls and mushroom satay are priced around the £4 mark, and most curries are about a fiver. The house wine is £8.50 a bottle. / 11.30 pm; closed Sun L.

Le Sacré-Coeur N1 £17   Ⓐ★
18 Theberton St   0171-354 2618   8–3D
This Islington spot has much of the spirit of a real Gallic bistro, and it's very popular locally thanks to its unpretentious approach and its reasonable prices. At lunchtime, the top-value choice is the 2-course set menu for £5.50 (3-courses £6.95), which offers such hearty choices as courgette soup, chicken chasseur and crème brûlée. A la carte, you would spend rather more, but still keep, without too much difficulty, within our budget. The house wine is £7.95 a bottle. / 11 pm.

St John EC1 £14* ★
26 St John St   0171-251 0848   9–1B
This converted Smithfield smokehouse has quite a following, thanks to its imaginative and honest cooking, but be warned that it is no place for veggies or those of a squeamish disposition – offal is the speciality. A la carte it's out of our price range, but the bar snacks offer a great introduction to their approach – you might try roast bone marrow and parsley salad (£5.80), or, for a less carnivorous bite, a cheese and chutney sandwich (£3.50). House wine is £11 a bottle, or drink 6X at £2.35 a pint. / 11.30 pm; closed Sun.

Sarastro WC2 £20*   Ⓐ
126 Drury Ln   0171-836 0101   2–2D
To be frank, you'd probably spend more than our price-limit at this popular Theatrelander (though it is possible to stay within it). So the food must be pretty special, right? Absolutely not – the cooking (vaguely Turkish, as if anyone cared) is by far the least of the attractions of this bizarre place, the theatricality of whose interior far outweighs anything likely to be on offer at the relaunched Royal Opera House. So for a loud party night out – or, curiously perhaps, a romantic meal on a budget – the place has a lot to commend it. The house wine is £9.75 a bottle. / 11.30 pm.

Sarcan N1 £14 ★
4 Theberton St   0171-226 5489   8–3D
Just off Islington's trendy Upper Street, this simple Turkish bistro offers reliable, inexpensive fare, such as borek (savoury pastries, £2.45) followed by diced lamb with aubergine and green pepper salad (£6.50). The house wine is £7.95 a bottle. / Midnight.

Satsuma W1 £15   𝔸
56 Wardour St   0171-437 8338   3–2D
You might not know this was a Japanese place from its name or its décor, but this stylish refectory-style Soho newcomer is perfect for those not very familiar with the cuisine. The bento boxes (£8.90-£12.90), for example, are traditional complete meals including some sort of protein (perhaps chicken deep-fried in breadcrumbs) together with boiled rice, some bite-size side-dishes, miso soup and pickles. House wine is £8.50 a bottle. / 11 pm; no smoking; no booking.

Scoffers SW11 £17   𝔸★
6 Battersea Rs   0171-978 5542   10–2C
This twentysomething Battersea hang-out clearly has a strong following and the crowd it attracts on a weekend makes booking a necessity. A pleasant, airy setting is much of the attraction, but there's also the reliable realisation of starters such as Thai fishcakes (£4.35), and main courses such as spinach, bacon and avocado salad (£6.95) or more meaty dishes for around a tenner. The house wine is £8.25 a bottle. / 11 pm.

Seafresh SW1 £13 ★
80-81 Wilton Rd   0171-828 0747   2–4B
It's not exactly in its first flush of youth, but this large Pimlico chippy offers a good range of dishes in a reassuringly traditional atmosphere. Fish soup (£3.35) is recommended, and to follow you might have, say, Scottish salmon cutlet (£7.95), or there are always specials of the day. The house wine is £7.65 a bottle. / 10.30 pm; closed Sun.

Seashell NW1 £15 ★★
49 Lisson Grove   0171-723 8703   8–4A
It has its ups and downs, but this famous (if dowdy) chippy near Marylebone Station can still offer top value, especially if you visit before 7pm, when you can have soup, fish 'n' chips, pudding and coffee, all for only £9.50. After that time, the main dish alone will cost you not much less. The house wine is £9 a bottle. / 10.30 pm; closed Sun D; no smoking area; no booking.

Shampers W1 £19 Ⓐ
4 Kingly St   0171-437 1692   3–2D
There are not many places in town where dinner is cheaper than lunch – this wine bar, only five minutes' walk from Piccadilly Circus, is one such place, and well worth bearing in mind if you're spending a night in the West End. With its haphazardly arranged paintings interspersed with wine racks, it looks rather dated – but in a characterful way – and the fare is suitably traditional. You might have grilled sardines (£4.50) followed by a casserole (£7.95), washed down with house wine at £10.50 a bottle. / 11 pm; closed Sun (Aug also Sat).

Shanghai E8 £16 ★
41 Kingsland High Street   0171-254 2878   1–1C
It's worth making a trek to this East End Chinese, whose premises used to house London's most famous pie 'n' eel shop and have been impressively restored (make sure you sit in the boothed section at the front). The top-value deal is the 3-course lunch and dinner (£10.50, Mon-Sat), which includes mixed starters, crispy aromatic duck, beef and chicken. Alternatively, at lunch, choose from the long and interesting menu of dim sum – most dishes are a couple of pounds, and the staff give helpful advice. The house wine is £7.50 a bottle.
/ 11 pm; no Amex.

The Ship SW18 £17 Ⓐ
41 Jews Row   0181-870 9667   10–2B
The main problem with this Wandsworth riverside pub is that on a sunny day – when there's a (not inexpensive) barbecue – every twentysomething in south west London seems to be crowded onto the terrace. All year round, though, good-quality, quite ambitious pub food is offered, such as smoked haddock fishcakes (£4.75) and chicken with mushroom compote and sage mash (£8). The house wine is £8.50 a bottle, or there's a good range of beers, including Young's Special at £2 a pint.
/ 10.30 pm; no booking for Sun L.

Le Shop SW3 £14 Ⓐ
329 King's Rd   0171-352 3891   5–3C
This attractive Chelsea crêperie – complete with booming classical 'background' music – is a welcome fixture in an ever-trendier part of town. It offers a wide range of pancake temptations both sweet and savoury, generally priced around the £3 mark. Salad niçoise (£6) is typical of the relatively few non-crêpe options. The house wine is £9 a bottle. / Midnight; no Switch.

Shree Krishna SW17 £12 ★★
192-194 Tooting High St   0181-672 4250   10–2D
It may not be an exciting place to look at, but if it's bang for your buck you're after, you won't do much better than this mainly vegetarian Tooting South Indian. Starters (around £2) are a special strength, and all the main dishes are £3.55. The house wine is £8 a bottle. / Mon-Thu 10.45 pm, Fri & Sat 11.45 pm; no Switch.

Silks & Spice £17 -
23 Foley St, W1   0171-636 2718   2–1B
95 Chiswick High Rd, W4   0181-995 7991   7–2B
28 Chalk Farm Road, NW1   0171-267 5751   8–2B
103 Boundary Road, NW8   0171-624 1485   8–3A
In our view, it's the lively atmosphere which lies at the roots of the success of this small Thai/Malaysian chain of restaurants, although the food is generally of a pretty good standard, too. At lunch, there's a one-plate special (£5.50) and a 3-course set menu (£12, including tea or coffee). A la carte, curries are generally around the £6 mark, and the house wine is £9.50 a bottle. / 11 pm; W1 closed Sat L & Sun L; no smoking areas.

Simpson's of Cornhill EC3 £15 𝔸★
38 1/2 Cornhill   0171-626 9985   9–2C
Probably the closest approximation to how it felt to eat in London two hundred years ago is to be found at this splendid chop-house, hidden away off a City back-alley. Thanks to its great character and minimal prices, younger bankers and stockbrokers are still happy to queue for such solid delights as pork chops or steak and kidney pie (both around a fiver), washed down by house wine at £10 a litre. This is such a time-bubble, you can even finish with a savoury – stewed cheese (£2.75) is recommended. / L only; closed Sat & Sun; no booking.

Smokey Joe's SW18 £16 ★
131 Wandsworth High St   0181-871 1785   10–2B
This tiny, quirky Caribbean diner in Wandsworth enjoys a disproportionate reputation thanks to the quality of its cooking. Peppered prawns (£3.40) followed by jerk chicken with red beans and rice (£7.75) are the sort of fare you might expect, and the BYO policy helps keep costs down. / 10 pm; closed Sun L; no credit cards; no booking.

Sofra £19 -
1 St Christopher's Pl, W1   0171-224 4080   3–1A
18 Shepherd Mkt, W1   0171-499 4099   3–4B
18 Shepherd St, W1   0171-493 3320   3–4B
17 Charing Cross Rd, WC2   0171-930 6090   4–4B
36 Tavistock St, WC2   0171-240 3773   4–3D
Offering essentially the same fare as their Café Sofra siblings, but in (slightly) more style and comfort, these Turkish/Lebanese restaurants are a handy, inexpensive central resource. The original branch, at Shepherd Market, has pleasant outside tables. Starters are all under a fiver, including the meze (£4.45), and mains cost £5.50-£7. The 'pre-recession' set menus (£5 lunch, £6.50 dinner), which give you a choice of one starter and one main course, are very good value. House wine is £10.35 a bottle. / Midnight.

Soho Brewing Company WC2 £17 -
41 Earlham St   0171-240 0606   4–2C
This hard-edged Covent Garden microbrewery comes as something of a surprise – for a trendy drinking place, the food is of good quality and sensibly priced, especially the lighter lunch options (mostly £5-£7). Evening choices include Toulouse sausage with bubble and squeak (£9.50), with all puddings, say, pear and chocolate tart, at £3.50. The house wine is relatively pricey, at £10.50 a bottle, or drink the homebrew at £2.80 a pint. / 11 pm.

Soho Spice W1 £18 ★★
124-126 Wardour St   0171-434 0808   3–1D
The buzzing atmosphere attests to the popularity of this brightly-hued modern curry house. Prices here are actually lower than they seem – there's a novelty – as each dish is in effect a set meal. Tandoori trout (£10.50), for example, comes with rice, vegetables of the day, lentils and a naan. There is also a 3-course pre-theatre menu (£8.50, 5pm-7pm). The catch is that wine prices kick off at £11.50 a bottle, and even beers are aggressively priced (large Cobra, £4.95), but at least the bar here goes on serving till 3 am (Fri & Sat).
/ 11.30 pm; 3 am Fri & Sat; no smoking area; need 4+ at L, 6+ at D to book.

Soulard N1 £20* 𝔸★
113 Mortimer Rd   0171-254 1314   1–1C
Philippe the happy proprietor can make a visit to this obscurely located Islington-fringe bistro seem quite an occasion. As you might expect, the real French cooking only just squeaks within our budget, but for your £14.95 you might have the likes of hot goat's cheese in honeyed breadcrumbs followed by rib-eye with Dijon mustard. Before 8.30pm (Tue-Thu) a pudding is even thrown in free. The house wine is £9.50 a bottle. / 10.30 pm; D only, closed Sun & Mon; no Switch.

Southeast W9 £16 ★
239 Elgin Avenue   0171-328 8883   1–2B
Both décor and service are on the sparse side at this small Maida Vale café. The cooking is spicy and accomplished South East Asian fare – a typical meal would start with deep-fried prawn and sweetcorn cake (£4.95), followed by a green chicken curry or a noodle dish (for around £7). House wine will set you back £9.95 a bottle. / 11 pm; no smoking area.

Spago SW7 £13 ★
6 Glendower Pl   0171-225 2407   5–2B
A convenient location, a couple of minutes' walk from South Kensington tube, helps make this unpretentious spot worth knowing about in this pricey area. No-nonsense classic Italian fare is the stock-in-trade, with the emphasis on pizza and pasta dishes (both around the £7 mark). The house wine is £5.60 for half a litre. / 12.30 am; D only; no credit cards.

La Spiga W1 £19 ★
84-86 Wardour Street   0171-734 3444   3–2D
As it's sited over Soho's ultra-hip K Bar, you might assume that this smart Italian sacrifices substance for style. Surprisingly, it doesn't, and the food is reasonably priced and interesting – a starter of Italian salami and fennel salad (£4.50) could be followed by angel hair pasta with prawns and chilli (£8.50), or one of the vast pizzas (£7-£9). House wine is £10.50 a bottle. / 11 pm; Midnight Thu-Sat; no smoking.

La Spighetta W1 £17 ★
43 Blandford St   0171-486 7340   2–1A
It may be rather lacking in traditional Italian warmth, but this bleakly furnished (and, in the basement, rather percussive) place offers good cooking in the thinly provided area around Baker Street. Pasta (around £9) and pizza (around £7.50) make up most of the menu, and the house wine is £9.50 a bottle. / 10.30 pm; no smoking area.

Sporting Page SW10 £16 🄰
6 Camera Pl   0171-376 3694   5–3B
This modern-style Chelsea boozer is the Front Page's racier twin, and offers similarly honest, but not especially adventurous dishes such as hot chicken salad, pasta of the week or salmon fishcakes (all priced around the £5.50-£7 mark). The house wine is £10 a bottle, or drink Courage bitter at £2.10 a pint. / 10 pm; no booking.

Sri Siam W1 £19* ★
16 Old Compton St   0171-434 3544   4–2A
The cooking at this large, stylishly minimal Soho ethnic provides a benchmark amongst London's Thai restaurants. The cheapest set menu is £12.95 – as a starter you might choose the Sri Siam selection followed by fried beef with ginger, which comes with vegetables, noodles and rice. You would need to take reasonable care to dine here within our budget, but, with most main dishes around £7, and with house wine at £9.50 a bottle, it is possible. / 11.15 pm; closed Sun L.

The Stable SW13 £19   Ⓐ
39 Barnes High St   0181-876 1855   10–1A
It's no great shakes on the culinary front, but this comfortable Barnes pub, famed for its jazz, has a characterful rear extension where you can enjoy hearty fare at reasonable prices – for example roast tomato and goat's cheese salad (£4.50), which you could follow with a pasta dish (all around £8), or cheese fondue (£9). The house wine is £10 a bottle. / 11 pm; D only, closed Sun-Wed.

Standard Tandoori W2 £14 ★
21-23 Westbourne Grove   0171-229 0600   6–1C
The name could not be more appropriate for this large Bayswater Indian, as you would be hard pushed to find a more classic curry-house – it's a true survivor of the '60s. The secret of success has been consistent quality at reasonable prices – even today, most dishes are less than a fiver, and a bottle of house wine is £7.50. / 11.45 pm; no smoking area.

Star Café W1 £11   -
22 Gt Chapel St   0171-437 8778   3–1D
Trendy, all-hours Soho is surprisingly thinly provided with places for a restorative greasy breakfast, so you may find it worth the effort to winkle out this comfortable, if somewhat obscurely located caff. A full English extravaganza is £4.65, including coffee. You won't spend very much more on the omelettes, pastas and so on which are the stock-in-trade at other times of day, when house wine will set you back £8.50 a bottle. / 4 pm; closed Sat & Sun; no credit cards; no smoking area.

Starbucks £ 6 🅐
137 Victoria St, SW1   0171-233 5170   2–4B
14 James St, W1   0171-495 6680   3–1A
27 Berkeley St, W1   0171-629 5779   3–3C
3 Grosvenor St, W1   0171-495 5534   3–2B
34 Gt Marlborough St, W1   0171-434 0778   3–2C
357-359 The Strand, WC2   0171-836 5166   2–2D
51-54 Long Acre, WC2   0171-836 2100   4–2D
25a Kensington High Street, W8   0171-937 5446   5–1A
America's mega-chain of coffee bars recently gulped down home-grown Seattle Coffee, and is in the process of re-branding all its outlets. Devotees will notice little real change, as the fresh-coffee-and-snacks formula which proved so successful for Seattle is also at the heart of Starbucks' philosophy. Prices are high, but so is quality – coffees cost from £1.50, muffins and brownies between £1 and £2, with substantial sandwiches from £1.40. / 6 pm – 11 pm; some branches closed Sat and/or Sun; no Amex; no smoking indoors; no booking.

The Stepping Stone SW8 £19* 🅐★★
123 Queenstown Rd   0171-622 0555   10–1C
Though it's very reasonably priced, this stylish and welcoming modern British restaurant in Battersea is still rather out of our price-bracket most of the time. Weekday lunches are all the more worth seeking out, therefore – a 2-course set menu, which might be curried parsnip soup followed by roast cod with leeks and fennel, will set you back only £11.95. The house wine is £10.50 a bottle. / 11 pm, Mon 10.30 pm; closed Sat L & Sun D; no smoking area.

Stick & Bowl W8 £ 9 ★
31 Kensington High St   0171-937 2778   5–1A
You'll find it difficult to spend even half our budget at this basic and uncomfortable Chinese canteen opposite Kensington Gardens – which is undoubtedly why there is always a stream of shoppers and locals going in for a quick, cheap bite. Spring rolls (90p) could be followed by beef in black bean sauce (£4) and rice (£2.50), and washed down with house wine at £7.50 a bottle. / 11 pm; no credit cards.

Sticky Fingers W8 £ 17 🅐
1a Phillimore Gdns   0171-938 5338   5–1A
Rock 'n' roll bands come and go, and so do burger joints. Like the Rolling Stones, however, Bill Wyman's upmarket Kensington diner (adorned with his memorabilia) is showing unusual staying power – testament to the place's good atmosphere and its quite reliable cooking. Starters, all under £5, might include potato skins or BBQ ribs – follow with burgers, from basic (£7.95) to 'with everything' (£10.95), and drink the house wine (£9.45). There are kids' meals for around £4. / 11.30 pm; book L only.

Stock Pot £ 9 ★
40 Panton St, SW1 0171-839 5142 4–4A
18 Old Compton St, W1 0171-287 1066 4–2B
50 James St, W1 0171-486 9185 3–1A
273 King's Rd, SW3 0171-823 3175 5–3C
6 Basil St, SW3 0171-589 8627 5–1D
The '60's live on at these unpretentious bistros, which are all the more worth knowing about as the areas in which they are located tend to be anything but economical. Don't expect food much above school dinners standard, but when the 3-course evening menu is only £5.90 (and house wine is £6.45 a bottle) who can really complain? Your selection might be avocado and prawns, followed by a beef hot-pot, with syrup sponge and custard to finish. / 11 pm-Midnight; no credit cards; some branches have no smoking areas; booking restricted at some times.

Stone Mason's Arms W6 £ 16 ★
54 Cambridge Grove 0181-748 1397 7–2C
The location could be better – on a busy Hammersmith highway – but all that is forgotten once inside this popular gastropub. Choose from a blackboard menu, say, soup (£3) or Greek salad (£5) as a starter, with pasta (£5) or fishcakes (£7.50) to follow. House wine is £8.45, or drink Guinness at £2.40 a pint. / 10.15 pm.

The Sun & Doves SE5 £ 19 𝔸★
61 Coldharbour Ln 0171-733 1525 1–4C
This trendy Camberwell gastropub is a great hang-out both in winter and summer – inside, it's filled with local artists' work, and outside, there's a large garden. Not only that, but the modern British grub is accomplished and the welcome is friendly. Start with stuffed baby squid (£4.85), with, perhaps, roast pork and prune couscous (£9.50) to follow. House wine is £9.50 a bottle, or drink draught Guinness at £2.50 a pint. / 10.30 pm; closed Sat L; no Amex.

Sushi Wong W8 £ 15 -
38c Kensington Church St 0171-937 5007 5–1A
Welcoming staff and well cooked dishes attract the locals to this small, somewhat characterless Japanese diner in Kensington. The best deal is the set lunch for £10.90, for which you can have a choice of starter (such as Korean salad), a main course – which might be tempura or chicken teriyaki (all served with rice and miso soup) – and a dessert. House wine is £9.95 a bottle. / 10.30 pm; closed Sun L.

Sushi-Say NW2   £18   ★
33b Walm Ln   0181-459 7512   1–1A
The friendly welcome and accomplished fare make it worth the expedition to the depths of north London (well, Willesden Green) to find this estimable Japanese. Prices are not bargain-basement, but you could start with chicken yakitori or dumplings (both around £4), then go for the assorted sushi – 8 pieces for £11.10. House wine is £9 a bottle, or drink tea for £1.50. / 10.30 pm; D only; closed Mon; no Amex.

Tandoori Lane SW6   £16   ★
131a Munster Rd   0171-371 0440   10–1B
This superior curry house in deepest Fulham distinguishes itself with its atmospheric décor, very attentive service and reliable cooking. Starters are all around £3, and main courses, say, tandoori butter chicken, cost about £5.50-£7. A bottle of house wine costs £9.95. / 11 pm; no Amex.

Tawana W2   £16   ★
3 Westbourne Grove   0171-229 3785   6–1C
It's not wildly atmospheric, but this airy Thai restaurant, a few yards from Queensway, maintains a devoted local following by offering consistently good-quality cooking at reasonable prices. Two people might share mixed starters (£6.95), and then you might have spicy prawn soup (£3.95) and beef with basil (£5.25). House wine is £8.50 a bottle. / 11 pm.

The Terrace W8   £19*   A★★
33c Holland St   0171-937 3224   5–1A
A la carte it's quite beyond our budget, but for £12.50 you can enjoy a 2-course set lunch at this charming, small Kensington restaurant (which is especially nice in summer, when the eponymous outside seating comes into its own). You might have goat's cheese salad, followed by honey and soy glazed pork, and wash it all down with house wine at £11.50 per bottle. / 10.30 pm; closed Sun D.

Thai Bistro W4   £16   ★
99 Chiswick High Rd   0181-995 5774   7–2B
You'll have to share the long benches with strangers at this popular Chiswick refectory, whose Thai menu always offers regional specialities and a plethora of veggie options. It's worth the lack of privacy though, for quality grub at a fair price. Starters, including spring rolls and mushroom satay, are all priced around the £4 mark, with main courses a few pounds more – maybe red beef curry or pad Thai. The house wine is an unsporting £10.50 a bottle, so drink Thai beers at £2.25. / 11 pm; closed Tue L & Thu L; no Amex & no Switch; no smoking.

Thai Break W8 £18 ★
30 Uxbridge St   0171-229 4332   6–2B
From the outside, this ordinary-looking Thai restaurant, just off Notting Hill Gate, appears rather hum-drum. Actually, the cooking is enjoyable and spicy, and reasonably priced. Traditional starters are all around the £3-£4 mark, and pad Thai costs £5.60. House wine is £10 a bottle. / 11 pm; closed Sun L.

Thai Pot WC2 £19* -
1 Bedfordbury   0171-379 4580   4–4C
Hidden away behind the Coliseum, this is a useful spot either before a night at the opera or as a venue for a not-too-pricey central get-together. You would have to be fairly careful to stay within our budget, but if you start with the Thai Pot selection of starters (£8 for two people) followed by the likes of a traditional green curry (£5.75), it's perfectly feasible. The house wine is £8.50 a bottle. / 11.15 pm; closed Sun; no smoking area.

Thai Pot Express WC2 £15 ★
148 Strand   0171-497 0904   2–2D
The setting is perhaps a little more comfortable than the term 'Express' might imply, and this is a useful place to know about in the rather dead environs of the Aldwych. Vegetable spring rolls (£3) make a good appetiser, and for a main course you could go for the king prawns sautéed in garlic (£6.50). House wine is £8.50 a bottle. / 11.15 pm; closed Sun.

Tibetan Restaurant WC2 £12 -
17 Irving St   0171-839 2090   4–4B
A perfect escape from the hubbub of Leicester Square, these quirky and unpretentious first-floor premises offer unusual, earthy dishes at low prices. Newcomers to the delights of Tibetan cuisine will find the staff eager to assist. You might try momo – steamed dumplings with a fiery sauce (£5.20) – or beef sha-balbe (£5.20), washed down the with house red wine at £7.95 a bottle. / 10.30 pm; closed Mon L & Sun; no Amex & no Switch.

Titanic W1 £19* ★
Regent Palace Hotel   0171-437 1912   3–3D
False expectations lead to disappointment, and if you think that Marco Pierre White's inolvement with this enormous brasserie near Piccadilly Circus means it will be wildly glamorous, think again. If you go expecting good nosh at reasonable prices, however, you'll probably enjoy the experience. Starters are expensive, so go for a main course (mostly £8-£10) such as 'hamburger à la McDonalds' or teriyaki salmon, with a pudding of, say, treacle sponge and custard (£3.50). House wine is £11 a bottle. / 11.30 pm.

Toff's N10 — £18 ★★
38 Muswell Hl Broadway   0181-883 8656   1–1B
Mercifully, a change of ownership has done little to dent the popularity of this Muswell Hill chippy, which continues to offer large portions of some of the very best fish 'n' chips in town. The set meal, available all day until 5pm, is the best value – £8.95 buys soup of the day, cod and chips, ice cream and tea or coffee. At other times, the main dish will set you back about the same amount. House wine comes reasonably priced at £8.75 a litre. / 10 pm; closed Mon & Sun; no booking.

Tokyo Diner WC2 — £11 ★
2 Newport Pl   0171-287 8777   4–3B
Sinophobe in Chinatown? – head for this efficiently run Japanese diner where a top-value weekday set lunch (£5.50) is among the attractions. Other recommendations include donburi – a single course meal in a box (£6.50) – as well as bento box meals (from £9.50) and generous sushi options from £6.50. The house wine is £6.90 a bottle. / Midnight; no Amex; no smoking area; Fri & Sat no booking.

Tom's W10 — £12   A★
226 Westbourne Grove   0171-221 8818   6–1B
If you want to hang out with the beautiful people of Notting Hill, this deli/café is one of the more affordable options. A toasted baguette with crispy bacon, tomato and Gruyère (£5.75) is a good example of what has become a house speciality, or you might go for the likes of roast vegetable and goat's cheese salad (£6.50). It's not really the sort of place where you would want to drink alcohol, but you can BYO if you want to. / L only (until 5 pm); no Amex; no smoking; no booking.

Topsy-Tasty W4 — £14 ★★
5 Station Parade   0181-995 3407   1–3A
Smarter and better value than its more famous sibling, the Bedlington Café, this '50s tea-room-style café, by Chiswick station, serves up some similarly notable Thai cooking. Most main dishes, such as chicken with sweet basil, are under a fiver and you could kick off with the likes of spring rolls (£3.20). You can BYO for modest corkage (80p a head). / 10.30 pm; D only; closed Sun; no credit cards.

Townhouse Brasserie WC1 — £17* ★
24 Coptic St   0171-636 2731   2–1C
The cooking doesn't strive to be remarkable, but this attractively housed establishment near the British Museum offers notably fair value, especially thanks to the all-day set menu. Your 2-course selection (£9.95) might be mussels in tomato and garlic, followed by roast chicken with mushrooms. Beware, though – house wine (at £11 a bottle) and eating à la carte are both relatively pricey. / 11.30 pm; no smoking area.

Troubadour SW5 £10 𝔸★
265 Old Brompton Rd   no tel   5–3A
This long-established Earl's Court coffee-shop is one of the few with a truly interesting interior, and it's long been the haunt of south west London's soi-disant intellectuals. New management are shaking off the rather grudging image the place used to convey, and it now offers quite good hot specials, such as sausage and mash (£4.50) with a glass of house wine (£1.50), as well as the coffee, cakes and breakfasts which have long been its stock-in-trade. / 10.30 pm; no credit cards; no booking.

Two Brothers N3 £18 ★★
297-303 Regent's Pk Rd   0181-346 0469   1–1B
We find it a touch characterless ourselves, but this airy North Finchley chippy certainly has a big north London following for the quality of its cooking. It's not especially cheap – cod 'n' chips are £8.65 (in the evenings) and house wine £8.75 a bottle. / 10.15 pm; closed Mon & Sun; no smoking area; book L only.

The Union Café W1 £15* -
96 Marylebone Ln   0171-486 4860   3–1A
If you're looking for lunch in a light and unpretentious setting then look no further than this Marylebone café-cum-restaurant – a plate of charcuterie (£7), washed down by house wine at £7.50 a bottle, is probably the sort of meal that shows the place to best advantage. You could easily overspend our budget if you went for the pricier items on the menu – one of the reasons why evening visits hold less attraction. / 10.30 pm; closed Sun; no Amex; no smoking area.

Uno SW1 £16 ★
1 Denbigh St   0171-834 1001   2–4B
Chic and modern, if crowded and noisy, this Pimlico Italian makes a very useful standby in a not overprovided part of town. Starters include the likes of deep-fried Mozzarella in sweet tomato sauce (£5.30), and for a main course, you'd have to stick to the pizzas or pastas (around £6) to keep within our budget. The house wine is £8 a bottle. / 11.15 pm; closed Sun; no credit cards.

Upper Street Fish Shop N1 £16 ★
324 Upper St   0171-359 1401   8–2D
This cosy Islington spot (known to its intimates as 'Olga's') is more a fish bistro than a chippy. So, though you can have good cod 'n' chips (£7.50), it's probably better to make a real meal of it. This is a BYO place, so take your own bottle of Chablis to wash down a fish soup (£3), followed by one of the more ambitious dishes such as fish lasagne (£9.50) or lemon sole stuffed with scallops (£10). / 10.15 pm; closed Mon L & Sun; no credit cards; no booking.

Veeraswamy W1 £17* 🅐★
Victory House, 101 Regent St   0171-734 1401   3–3D
This very central site may claim to house the oldest Indian restaurant in London (1927), but you wouldn't know it from its bright and zingy décor which is very much of the '90s. The innovative cooking is well outside our budget most of the time, but, pre-theatre (5.30pm-6.30pm) there's a good-value set dinner (£11). The house wine is £10.95 a bottle.
/ 11.30 pm; Sun 10 pm; closed Sun.

The Vegetarian Cottage NW3 £17 -
91 Haverstock Hl   0171-586 1257   8–2B
Here's your chance to visit a real speciality restaurant – a Chinese veggie. Some feel the results are on the bland side, but you get quite a lot for your money – the £13.50 set menu, for example, includes mixed starter, hot and sour soup, lotus leaf-wrapped vegetables, sweet and sour beancurd, noodles and special fried rice. The house wine is a modest £7.90 a bottle. / 11.15 pm; D only ex Sun open L & D; no Amex.

Le Versailles SW9 £18* ★
20 Trinity Gdns   0171-326 0521   10–2D
We find this Gallic bistro in Brixton a touch challenged in the atmosphere department, but it undoubtedly offers good value if you stick to the set menus, especially early in the week. Mon-Thu, a 3-course set dinner will set you back £10 (£13.50, Fri & Sat) – you might have fish soup, followed by fishcakes and chocolate tart. The house wine is £9.95 a bottle. / 10.30 pm, Fri & Sat 11 pm; closed Mon; no Amex; no smoking area.

Vijay NW6 £12 ★
49 Willesden Ln   0171-328 1087   1–1B
Nothing will break the bank at this weatherbeaten Kilburn Indian stalwart of over two decades' standing. The menu combines interesting southern Indian vegetarian specialities (vegetable korma at £2.50, coconut rice costs £1.95) with more standard meat curries curries (all of which are around £4). Drink Kingfisher (£3), or the house wine (£8). / 10.45 pm, Fri & Sat 11.45 pm; no Amex.

Vincent's SW15 £17* ★
147 Upper Richmond Rd   0181-780 3553   10–2B
This jolly and welcoming suburban bistro, decorated in homage to Van Gogh, is a rightly popular Putney standby. Two-course set menus at both lunch (£7.95) and dinner (£9.50) are a key attraction for the budget diner – you might start with the likes of bacon and avocado salad, followed by salmon en croûte. The house wine is £9.95 a bottle. / 10.30 pm; closed Sat L & Sun, open Sun L in winter; no smoking area.

The Vine NW5 £19* ★
86 Highgate Rd   0171-209 0038   8–1B
This Kentish Town gastropub is notable for its pleasant garden, laid-back approach and generous portion control. You will need to choose carefully from the menu, as some dishes are pricey – a starter of caramelised red onion tart (£5.45), followed by tagliatelle with roast tomatoes and Tallegio cheese (£8.95) might fit the bill – and a bottle of house wine is £9.95. / 10 pm; closed Mon L; no smoking area.

Vingt-Quatre SW10 £17   Ⓐ
325 Fulham Rd   0171-376 7224   5–3B
The trendy stretch of pavement on the fringe of Chelsea christened 'The Beach' by certain style-mags is home to this useful 24-hour diner, which serves up simple fare to the local gilded youth. Starters might include broccoli and Stilton soup (£3.25) or calamari (£4.75), and main courses, such as fishcakes, Cumberland sausages and fillet steak all cost between £7 and £10. Puddings, like banoffi pie, are £3.75, and house wine is £9.95 a bottle. / open 24 hours; no booking.

Vrisaki N22 £18 ★
73 Myddleton Rd   0181-889 8760   1–1C
If you have a boundless appetite, this large Bounds Green Greek is the place for you. From our experience, you are unlikely to be able to finish the enormous set meze – which will set you back £28 for two people, with house wine at £8.50 a bottle. / Midnight; closed Sun; no Amex.

Wagamama £12 ★
101 Wigmore Street, W1   0171-409 0111   3–1A
10a Lexington St, W1   0171-292 0990   3–2D
4a Streatham St, WC1   0171-323 9223   2–1C
The London originators of the no-frills, refectory-style oriental noodle-bar revolution remain in its vanguard, and these establishments' popularity is such that you may well have to queue. The top-of-the-range choice is an 'Absolute Wagamama' – chicken ramen, 3 gyoza (dumplings) and a Kirin beer – which will set you back all of £8.50. The new branch in Wigmore Street recently opened, with a café attached. / 11 pm; no smoking; no booking.

Weng Wah House NW3 £15 ★
240 Haverstock Hl   0171-794 5123   8–2A
This Belsize Park fixture offers good Chinese cooking at modest prices in comfortable and quite stylish surroundings. It's not meant as a criticism to say the long menu is fairly standard. Many main courses are priced around the £6 mark, and wine prices kick off at £8.90 a bottle. Top tip for value is the 2-course set lunch (£4.80). / 11.30 pm; no Amex.

West End Kitchen SW1 £ 8 -
5 Panton St   0171-839 4241   4–4A
This cramped, friendly Haymarket canteen offers a 3-course set menu, which is some the best value you are likely to find hereabouts. There is plenty of choice and portions are generous. Your meal might consist of deep-fried mushrooms, chicken Kiev and apple crumble. The cooking has no pretensions to being a gourmet production, but with the menu costing £5.50 and a bottle of the house wine the same again, it's difficult to complain. / 11.45 pm.

The Westbourne W2 £ 15 𝔸
101 Westbourne Park Villas   0171-221 1332   6–1B
This converted pub is technically in Bayswater but Notting Hill's trustafarians have still adopted it as their spiritual home. It throbs with one of London's most interesting crowds, especially at weekends – on a sunny day, the terrace overflows as well. It's perhaps no surprise that the food and service can be erratic, but, on a good day, dishes such as lentil soup with egg pasta (£4) and seared scallops with sweet chilli sauce (£8.50) are well done. The house wine is £8.50, but the trendy drink Leffe Belgian beer at £2.10 a half-pint.
/ 10 pm; closed Mon L; no Amex.

White Cross Hotel TW9 £ 14 𝔸
Water Ln   0181-940 6844   1–4A
This impressive pub makes an agreeable Richmond destination both in winter (when there are roaring fires) and summer (when you can enjoy a river-view from the beer garden). The menu isn't ambitious – French onion soup (£3.25) followed by pork chops with tarragon sauce (£6.25), would be a typical choice, and the bar menu offers staples such as ploughman's lunches and jacket potatoes, for under a fiver. The house wine is £9.50 a bottle. / L only; no Amex; no booking.

Windsor Castle W8 £ 13 𝔸
114 Campden Hl Rd   0171-243 9551   6–2B
Few other pubs in London match this quaint, but untouristy Georgian tavern (named for its now obscured westerly views), which combines rambling, cosy charm with good beer and enjoyable pub-grub. Starters range from chips 'n' dips (£2.95) to oysters (£6), and for a main dish you could have fishcakes (£6.25) or lamb with roasted vegetables (£7.25). House wine is £11.95 a bottle, but most people opt for a pint (London Pride is £2.25 a pint). / 10.30 pm; no smoking area (L only); no booking.

Wine & Kebab SW10 £20* -
343 Fulham Rd   0171-352 0967   5–3B
Those in search of a filling dinner on the Fulham-ward fringe of Chelsea late at night don't have an embarrassment of choice. It's worth remembering, then, this long-established Greek place, where the mixed meze (£30 for two people) is the top-value choice, washed down by house wine at £8.50 a bottle. / 2 am; D only.

Wine Gallery SW10 £16   Ⓐ
49 Hollywood Rd   0171-352 7572   5–3B
If you like your wine, but can't really afford it, the enlightened low mark-up policy of this long-established Chelsea diner is especially attractive. The house wine is only £6 a bottle – and for the tenner a bottle no longer uncommon for house wines elsewhere, you could even aspire to the likes of 'Mad Fish' Australian Pinot Noir. The International menu is perhaps a lesser attraction, but – with all starters under a fiver and most mains well under a tenner – it's difficult to be too picky. There's also a nice garden, weather permitting. / 11.45 pm; no Amex.

Wódka W8 £17*   ★
12 St Alban's Grove   0171-937 6513   5–1B
Located in a charming Kensington backwater, this modern Polish restaurant (if that's not a contradiction in terms) serves a bargain set lunch, which provides the chance to eat on the cheap in a fashionable quarter. There are 2-course (£10.90) and 3-course (£13.90) options – you could start with mussels, follow with chicken Kiev and potato pancakes, and have crème brûlée for pudding. House wine is £9.90 a bottle.
/ 11.15 pm; closed Sat L & Sun L; smart casual.

Wolfe's WC2 £18   ★
30 Gt Queen St   0171-831 4442   4–1D
Decorated in a style that passed for very fashionable, circa 1975, this eminent Covent Garden diner retains a reputation as one of London's top spots for lovers of hamburgers (mostly £7-£8), and its comfortable and relaxed style makes it ideal for a family outing. The house wine is £8.75 a bottle.
/ 11.30 pm; closed Sun.

Wong Kei W1 £10 ★
41-43 Wardour St   0171-437 8408   4–3A
The fact that 'nice' is an epithet few would apply to this Chinatown behemoth does little to diminish its popularity. Devotees know the place offers good Cantonese chow cheaply – with most dishes under a fiver – and in copious quantities. Your food comes quickly, usually in the right order, and – if you are very lucky – with the peculiar absence of grace long regarded as the place's special hallmark. To obtain the full benefit, try paying in something other than hard cash.
/ 11.30 pm; no credit cards; no booking.

Woodlands £10* -
37 Panton St, SW1   0171-839 7258   4–4A
77 Marylebone Ln, W1   0171-486 3862   3–1A
They're rather pricey à la carte, but the lunchtime buffets (£5.99) at these vegetarian Indians (one of which has a very central West End location, just off the Haymarket) offer good value. The house wine is £8.50 a bottle. / 10.30 pm.

Yas W14 £15 -
7 Hammersmith Rd   0171-603 9148   7–1D
This reliable Persian, opposite Olympia, particularly comes into its own in the wee hours – it's one of the best late night options for miles around. Everything comes in generous portions – all the starters, such as garlicky lentils in yoghurt and feta, are £3.50, and mains include lamb and kidney bean stew (£7). House wine (during licensed hours) is £9 a bottle.
/ 5 am; no Amex.

Yo! Sushi W1 £16 Ⓐ
52-53 Poland St   0171-287 0443   3–1D
Hi-tech is the gimmick at this fun Soho sushi bar – press a button for service, and get your drinks from robotic trollies. The food? – that comes by conveyor-belt (of course), and you know the price of each of the 180 dishes (£1.50-£3.50) from the colour-coding of the plates. The house wine is £12 a bottle, so drink sake at £3. / Midnight; no smoking; no booking.

Yoshino W1 £18 ★
3 Piccadilly Pl   0171-287 6622   3–3D
Everyone who fancies themselves as a connoisseur of sushi, should pay a visit to this minimalist café – in an alleyway between Piccadilly and Regent Street. Brave yourself for the lack of any menu in English, so if your Japanese is less than fluent, be prepared to bluff, and accept whatever you are given. There's no wine or coffee, so drink the sake, from £4 a pot. / 9 pm; closed Sun; no smoking area.

Yum Yum N16 £17 ★
30 Stoke Newington Ch St 0171-254 6751 1–1C
Thanks to its reliable cooking, this ornately decorated Thai restaurant in Stoke Newington is one of the longer-running success-stories – even in a part of town where there's ever more competition. Top value is the 2-course set lunch menu (£6.95), which might include tom yam (hot and sour soup with lemon-grass), followed by duck curry. Even à la carte, though, and with house wine at £8.95 a bottle, you can eat within our budget at any time. / *10.45 pm, Fri & Sat 11.15 pm.*

Zamoyski NW3 £15 -
85 Fleet Rd 0171-794 4792 8–2A
In most Eastern European restaurants, copious vodka consumption is a major part of the attraction. This quirky West Hampstead spot admirably lives up to its origins, and if you visit before 7pm, shots will set you back only £1.25 each. Culinarily, the highlight is the 9-course meze special (£6.50), or there are robust single dishes such as sauerkraut and mushroom pie, for about the same amount. The house wine is £9.25 a bottle. / *11 pm; D only ex Sun, when open all day; no Amex & no Switch; smart casual.*

Zed SW2 £15 𝔸
30 Acre Ln 0171-501 9001 10–2D
A useful addition to Brixton's up-and-coming restaurant scene, this fun bar-café has a friendly attitude and is a particular choice for summer, when the (slightly trafficky) outside terrace comes into its own. A typical starter would be goat's cheese cake with spicy plum relish (£3.80), and the best bet for a main dish is one of the tasty pizzas (£6.50) – a greater attraction than the rather indifferent pasta (at a similar price). House wine is £9.80 a bottle. / *11 pm; closed Mon.*

ZeNW3 NW3 £18* 𝔸★
83 Hampstead High St 0171-794 7863 8–2A
The minimalist, modern design of this impressively glazed Chinese restaurant – all the more notable for being located in the heart of historic Hampstead – has stood the test of time and makes a pleasant venue for its good quality set lunch (£12.50). You might have mixed hors d'oeuvres, soup and crispy aromatic duck. With house wine at £12 a bottle, you would have difficulty keeping within our budget at other times. / *11.30 pm; smart casual.*

INDEXES

INDEXES

Breakfast
(with opening times)

Central
Aurora *(8)*
Balans: *all branches (8)*
Bank *(7.30)*
Bar Italia *(7)*
Café Bohème *(8)*
Café Sofra: *all branches (7)*
Food for Thought *(9.30)*
Italian Kitchen *(10)*
Maison Bertaux *(9)*
Mediterranean Café *(8)*
Museum St Café *(8)*
Pâtisserie Valerie: *Old Compton St W1 (7.30, Sun 9); RIBA Centre, 66 Portland Pl W1 (8); Marylebone High St W1 (8, Sun 9); WC2 (9.30, Sun 9)*
Pizza On The Park *(8.30)*
Pret A Manger: *Tottenham Court Rd W1 (7.15); Victoria St SW1, Marylebone High St W1, High Holborn WC1 (7.30); Baker St W1 (7.45); Kingsgate Pd, Victoria St SW1, Regents St W1, Oxford St W1, Wardour St W1, Hanover St W1, Piccadilly W1, High Holborn WC1, WC2 (7.30)*
Star Café *(7.30)*
Stock Pot: *SW1 (7); James St W1 (8)*
The Union Café *(Mon-Fri 9.30)*
West End Kitchen *(7)*

West
Balans West: *all branches (8)*
Bedlington Café *(8)*
Beirut Express *(9.30)*
Brass. du Marché *(10, Sun 11)*
Café 206 *(8)*
Café Grove *(9.30)*
Café Montpeliano *(8)*
Chelsea Kitchen *(8)*
Coins *(8.30, Sun 10)*
The Crescent *(11)*
Ed's Easy Diner: *SW3 (Sat & Sun 9)*
Fat Boy's *(7)*
Fileric *(8)*
Francofill *(Sat & Sun 10)*
Ghillies: *SW6 (9)*
King's Road Café *(10)*
Lisboa Patisserie *(8)*
Manzara *(7.30)*
Le Metro *(7.30, Sun 8.30)*
Mona Lisa *(7)*
Pâtisserie Valerie: *SW3 (7.30, Sun 9)*
Pret A Manger: *W8 (7.30); SW3, W6 (8)*
Ranoush *(9)*
Raoul's Café *(9, Sun 9.30)*
Riccardo's *(8)*
Le Shop *(Sat & Sun 11)*
Stock Pot: *Basil St SW3 (7.30); King's Rd SW3 (7.45)*
Tom's *(8)*
Troubadour *(8.30)*
Vingt-Quatre *(24 hr)*

North
Bar Gansa *(10.30)*
Café Mozart *(9)*
Ed's Easy Diner: *NW3 (Sat & Sun 9)*
Iznik *(Sat & Sun 9)*
Nontas *(8)*
Pret A Manger: *NW1 (6); N1 (8)*

South
Alma *(Sat & Sun 10)*
Boiled Egg *(9, Sun 10)*
Café de la Place *(8, Sat 9, Sun 9.30)*
Café Portugal *(10)*
Gastro *(8)*
Hornimans *(Sun 8)*
Pizzeria Franco *(9)*
Scoffers *(10.30, Sat & Sun 10)*

East
Brick Lane Beigel Bake *(24 hr)*
Café Sofra: *all branches (7)*
Carnevale *(10)*
Fox & Anchor *(7)*
Frocks *(Sat & Sun 11)*
Futures *(7.30)*
Futures *(7.30)*
Hope & Sir Loin *(7)*
Lunch *(8.30)*
The Place Below *(7.30)*
Pret A Manger: *both EC2 (7); EC1, EC4 (7.30)*

BYO
(Bring your own wine)

Central
Food for Thought
Fryer's Delight
India Club
Neal's Yard Dining Rooms

West
Adams Café
Alounak
Bedlington Café
Blah! Blah! Blah!
Fat Boy's
Fats
El Gaucho
Kalamaras, Micro
Mandola
Tom's
Topsy-Tasty
Yas

INDEXES

North
Ali Baba
Diwana Bhel-Poori House
Upper St Fish Shop

South
Monsieur Max
Pizzeria Franco

East
Lahore Kebab House

Children

(h – high or special chairs
m – children's menu
p – children's portions
e – weekend entertainments
o – other facilities)

Central
Alfred (hp)
Ask! Pizza: all branches (hp)
Balans: W1 (p)
Bank (hp)
Blues (o)
Boudin Blanc (h)
Café Emm (h)
China City (h)
Chuen Cheng Ku (h)
Ed's Easy Diner: Trocadero W1 (hm); Moor St W1 (m)
Efes Kebab House: Great Titchfield St W1 (h); Gt Portland St W1 (hp)
Golden Dragon (h)
Gourmet Pizza Co.: all branches (hm)
Hamine (p)
Harbour City (h)
Hard Rock Café (hmpo)
Italian Kitchen (mo)
Joy King Lau (h)
Little Havana (e)
Maroush: all branches (p)
Matsuri (m)
Mayflower (h)
Mediterranean Café (hp)
Melati (h)
New World (h)
Pizza On The Park (h)
PizzaExpress: all central branches (h)
Pizzeria Condotti (h)
Poons (h)
RK Stanleys (hp)
Royal China: all branches (hm)
Satsuma (h)
Seafresh (hp)
Silks & Spice: all branches (h)
Sofra: Shepherd St W1, St Christopher's Pl W1, both WC2 (h)
La Spiga (hp)
La Spighetta (hp)
Thai Pot (p)
Townhouse Brasserie (hm)
Wagamama: all branches (h)
Wolfe's (hm)
Woodlands: W1 (h)

West
The Abingdon (h)
Alounak (h)
Ask! Pizza: all branches (hp)
Balans West: SW5 (hp)
Bluebird (hm)
Blythe Road (p)
Brass. du Marché (hp)
Brilliant (p)
Chelsea Kitchen (p)
Chiswick (hp)
The Cross Keys (hm)
Da Mario (hmp)
Da Pierino (hm)
Daquise (p)
Ed's Easy Diner: SW3 (hm)
Fat Boy's (h)
Ffiona's (p)
Francofill (hp)
Galicia (p)
Geale's (h)
Ghillies: SW6 (p)
Halepi (p)
The Havelock Tavern (hp)
Isfehan (hpo)
Kalamaras, Micro (hp)
Khan's (h)
Khan's of Kensington (h)
King's Road Café (p)
Leonardo's (p)
Made in Italy (h)
Madhu's Brilliant (hp)
Malabar (hp)
Mandalay (p)
Mandarin Kitchen (h)
Manzara (h)
Maroush: all branches (p)
Mas Café (h)
Mona Lisa (p)
Nayab (h)
Palatino (hp)
PizzaExpress: SW10, both SW3, W11, W14, W2, W4, W8 (h); SW6 (ho)
Raoul's Café (h)
Riccardo's (o)
Royal China: all branches (hm)
Sabai Sabai (h)
Le Shop (hp)
Silks & Spice: all branches (h)
Sticky Fingers (hmeo)
Tom's (h)
Wine & Kebab (h)
Wine Gallery (p)
Yas (hp)

INDEXES

North
Ask! Pizza: *all branches (hp)*
Bu San *(h)*
Centuria *(h)*
Cucina *(h)*
Daphne *(p)*
Don Pepe *(hp)*
Ed's Easy Diner: NW3 *(hm)*
La Finca: *all branches (he)*
Florians *(hp)*
The Fox Reformed *(hpo)*
Frederick's *(hm)*
Great Nepalese *(p)*
Greek Valley *(hm)*
Gresslin's *(hpo)*
Kavanagh's *(p)*
Lansdowne *(h)*
Laurent *(p)*
The Little Bay *(h)*
Manna *(h)*
Mesclun *(p)*
Nautilus *(h)*
La Piragua *(h)*
PizzaExpress: *all north branches (h)*
La Porchetta Pizzeria *(h)*
Rani *(hm)*
Sarcan *(h)*
Seashell *(hm)*
Silks & Spice: *all branches (h)*
Upper St Fish Shop *(h)*
The Vegetarian Cottage *(h)*
Vijay *(h)*
The Vine *(p)*
Weng Wah House *(h)*
Yum Yum *(h)*
Zamoyski *(p)*

South
Alma *(p)*
Babur Brasserie *(h)*
Battersea Rickshaw *(hp)*
Boiled Egg *(hme)*
Brady's *(p)*
Buona Sera *(h)*
Café Portugal *(hp)*
Cantinetto Venegazzú *(hp)*
don Fernando's *(hp)*
Eco *(h)*
La Finca: *all branches (he)*
Gastro *(p)*
Ghillies: SW17 *(hp)*
Gourmet Pizza Co.: *all branches (hm)*
Heather's *(ho)*
Helter Skelter
The Honest Cabbage *(p)*
Hornimans *(hm)*
Kastoori *(p)*
La Lanterna *(h)*
The Lavender: SW11 *(p)*
La Mancha *(h)*
Monsieur Max *(m)*
Newton's *(hme)*
Ost. Antica Bologna *(p)*
Phoenix *(h)*
Pizza Metro *(h)*
PizzaExpress: *both SE1, Lavender Hill SW11, SW14, SW15, SW18 (h); Battersea Br Rd SW11, SW4 (ho)*
Pizzeria Castello *(h)*
Pizzeria Franco *(h)*
Le Pont de la Tour Bar & Grill *(h)*
Ransome's Dock *(hp)*
La Rueda *(hp)*
Scoffers *(hm)*
The Stepping Stone *(h)*
The Sun & Doves *(hp)*
White Cross Hotel *(h)*
Zed *(heo)*

East
Arkansas Café *(p)*
Ask! Pizza: *all branches (hp)*
Café Spice Namaste *(h)*
The Eagle *(p)*
Faulkner's *(h)*
Frocks *(hp)*
Futures *(p)*
Gourmet Pizza Co.: *all branches (hm)*
PizzaExpress: *all east branches (h)*
St John *(h)*
Shanghai *(hp)*

Entertainment
(Check times before you go)

Central
Blues
  (jazz, Fri & Sat)
Café Bohème
  (jazz, Tue-Sat)
Café Latino
  (music, Tue, Fri & Sat)
Calabash
  (African band, Fri or Sat)
Efes Kebab House: *Gt Portland St W1 (belly dancer, nightly)*
Hamine
  (karaoke, Mon-Sat)
Havana
  (DJ, nightly)
Ishbilia
  (music, Sat & Sun)
The Lexington
  (pianist, Tue-Fri)
Little Havana
  (DJ & dancing, nightly)
Pizza On The Park
  (jazz, nightly)
PizzaExpress
  Dean St W1 (jazz, nightly); Greek St W1 (jazz, Thu-Sat)

INDEXES

Sofra:
both WC2 (music, Mon-Sat)

West

Café O
(Greek music, Thu-Sat)
Chutney Mary
(jazz, Sun L)
Da Mario
(disco, nightly ex Sun)
Isfehan
(music, nightly)
Maroush
W2 (music & dancing, nightly)
Mas Café
(bands & party nights)
Patio
(gypsy music, nightly)
Pizza Pomodoro
(music, nightly)
PizzaExpress
W8 (jazz, Fri & Sat); W14 (jazz, Sat); Beauchamp Pl SW3 (jazz, Sat & Sun)
Wine & Kebab
(music, Sat)

North

Don Pepe
(singing & organist, nightly)
La Finca
N1 (rhumba & flamenco, Wed; salsa some Fri)
The Fox Reformed
(regular wine tasting and backgammon tournaments; book club)
Greek Valley
(bouzouki music, Fri)
PizzaExpress
Kentish Town Road NW1 (jazz, Tue & Thu eves)
Weng Wah House
(karoke, nightly)
Zamoyski
(Russian music, Fri & Sat)

South

La Finca
SE11 (Latin music, Sat)
Heather's
(jazz, first Tue of mo)
The Honest Cabbage
(pianist and singer)
Hornimans
(jazz, Sun; DJs Mon)
La Mancha
(guitar, nightly)
Meson don Felipe
(flamenco guitar, nightly)
PizzaExpress
SW18 (large sports TV)
Pizzeria Castello
(guitarist, nightly)
Le Pont de la Tour Bar & Grill *(jazz, nightly)*
Rebato's
(music, Wed-Sat)
La Rueda
(disco, Fri & Sat)
Zed
(jazz, Fri & Sat eves)

East

Barcelona Tapas
EC3 (magician, regularly; occasional flamenco)
Cantaloupe
(DJ's Wed & Sat pm)

Late

(open till midnight or later as shown; may be earlier Sunday)

Central

Balans: *W1 (Mon-Sat 3 am, Sun 1 am)*
Bar Italia *(4 am, Fri & Sat 24 hours)*
Blues *(Thu-Sat only)*
Brahms
Café Bohème *(2.45 am, Thu-Sat open 24 hours)*
Café du Jardin
Café Emm *(Fri & Sat 12.30 am)*
Café Latino *(Thu-Sat 1 am)*
Café Sofra: *all central branches*
Ed's Easy Diner: *all central branches (midnight, Fri & Sat 1 am)*
Efes Kebab House: *Gt Portland St W1 (Fri & Sat 3 am)*
Golden Dragon *(Fri & Sat only)*
Hamine *(2.30 am, Sat 1.30 am, Sun midnight)*
Hard Rock Café *(12.30 am, Fri & Sat 1 am)*
Hujo's
Ishbilia
Italian Kitchen
Maroush: *W1 (1 am)*
Mayflower *(3.45 am)*
Mediterranean Café *(midnight, Fri-Sat 1 am)*
Melati *(Fri & Sat 12.30 am)*
Mirabelle
Mr Kong *(2.45 am)*
Pizza On The Park
PizzaExpress: *SW1, Baker St W1, Bruton Pl W1, Upper St James Street W1, Dean St W1, Barrett St W1, Wardour St W1, WC1, both WC2; Greek St W1 (midnight, Wed-Sat 1 am)*
Pizzeria Condotti
Pollo
Sofra: *all branches*
Soho Spice *(3 am Fri & Sat)*
La Spiga *(Thu-Sat only)*
Tokyo Diner
Yo! Sushi

West

Alounak
Anarkali
Balans West: *SW5 (1 am)*
Beirut Express *(1.45 am)*
Bersagliera
La Delizia
Ed's Easy Diner: *SW3*
Halepi *(12.30 am)*

INDEXES

Isfehan
Lou Pescadou
Maroush: W2 (1.30 am); SW3 (5 am)
Nayab
Patio
Pizza Pomodoro (1 am)
PizzaExpress: SW10, both SW3, W11, W14, W2, W4, W8
Pucci Pizza (12.30 am)
Ranoush (3 am)
Riccardo's
Le Shop
Spago (12.30 am)
Wine & Kebab (2 am)
Yas (5 am)

North
Ali Baba
Anglo Asian Tandoori (Fri & Sat 12.15 am)
Bar Gansa
Don Pepe
Ed's Easy Diner: NW3
La Finca: N1 (1.30 am, Fri & Sat)
Greek Valley
The Little Bay
Pasha (Fri & Sat)
La Piragua
PizzaExpress: all north branches
La Porchetta Pizzeria
Rasa: N16 (Fri & Sat only)
Sarcan
Vrisaki

South
Buona Sera
Gastro
PizzaExpress: Lavender Hill SW11, SW14, SW15, SW18; Cardomom Bldg, Shad Thames SE1 (not Sun)

East
Brick Lane Beigel Bake (24 hr)
Cantaloupe

No-smoking areas
(* completely no smoking)

Central
Café Sofra: all branches
China City
Chuen Cheng Ku
Ed's Easy Diner: all branches
Food for Thought*
Gourmet Pizza Co.: W1
Goya
Hard Rock Café
Ikkyu: WC2
Maison Bertaux
Malabar Junction
Mandeer*
Mildreds*
Museum St Café*
Neal's Yard Dining Rooms*
Pizza On The Park
PizzaExpress: SW1
Poons, Lisle Street
Pret A Manger: both SW1, Regents St W1, Oxford St W1, Tottenham Court Rd W1, Wardour St W1, Hanover St W1, Piccadilly W1, Baker St W1, both WC1, WC2
Rasa: all branches*
Ristorante Italiano
RK Stanleys
Satsuma*
Silks & Spice: W1
Soho Spice
La Spighetta
Star Café
Thai Pot
Tokyo Diner
Townhouse Brasserie
The Union Café
Wagamama: Lexington St W1, WC1*
Yo! Sushi*
Yoshino

West
Chelsea Kitchen
Chutney Mary
Daquise
Ed's Easy Diner: all branches
Emile's: all branches
Fats*
Francofill
Khan's of Kensington
King's Road Café
Krungtap
Mandalay*
Manzara*
Palatino
The Papaya Tree
Patio
Pret A Manger: all west branches
Raoul's Café
S&P Patara: Beauchamp Pl SW3
Southeast
Standard Tandoori
Stock Pot: Basil St SW3
Thai Bistro*
Tom's*
Windsor Castle

North
Café Mozart*
Diwana Bhel-Poori House
Ed's Easy Diner: all branches
Frederick's
Gresslin's
Manna*
Pret A Manger: all north branches
Rani

INDEXES

Rasa: *all branches**
Seashell
Two Brothers
The Vine

South
The Apprentice
Babur Brasserie
Eco
Emile's: *all branches*
Gastro
Heather's*
Newton's
The Old School Thai
The Pepper Tree
The Stepping Stone
Le Versailles
Vincent's

East
Café Sofra: *all branches*
Cantaloupe
Futures
Futures*
Gourmet Pizza Co.: *E14*
Lunch*
Moshi Moshi Sushi: *EC2**
The Place Below*
Pret A Manger: *EC4*; EC1, both EC2*
Rupee Room

Outside tables
(* particularly recommended)

Central
Alfred
Andrew Edmunds
Ask! Pizza: *Grafton Way W1*
Aurora*
Bar Italia
Boudin Blanc*
Brahms*
Café Bohème
Café Coq
Café du Jardin
Café Emm
Café Latino
Café Sofra: *Shepherd Mkt W1*; Wigmore St W1, both WC2*
Ed's Easy Diner: *Moor St W1*
Efes Kebab House: *Great Titchfield St W1*
Gordon's Wine Bar*
Goya
Hard Rock Café
Hunan
Ishbilia
Italian Kitchen
Jenny Lo's
Little Havana
Maison Bertaux
Mediterranean Café
Mildreds
Mirabelle*
Momo
Museum St Café
Nine Golden Square
Noho
Pâtisserie Valerie: *RIBA Centre, 66 Portland Pl W1*; Marylebone High St W1, WC2*
Pizza On The Park
PizzaExpress: *Baker St W1, Charlotte St W1, Barrett St W1, WC1*
La Poule au Pot
Pret A Manger: *Regents St W1, Tottenham Court Rd W1, Marylebone High St W1, Baker St W1, both WC1, WC2*
Silks & Spice: *all branches*
Sofra: *St Christopher's Pl W1*; Shepherd St W1, Shepherd Mkt W1*
La Spighetta
Stock Pot: *both W1*
Townhouse Brasserie
Uno
Wolfe's

West
The Abingdon*
Anglesea Arms
Ask! Pizza: *W4*
Balans West: *SW5*
Bedlington Café
Blythe Road
Brass. du Marché
Café 206
Café Grove*
Café Montpeliano
Café O
Chelsea Kitchen
Chelsea Ram
Chiswick
Cibo
Coins*
Costa's Grill*
Coyote Café*
Da Pierino
Dove
Elistano
Emile's: *SW6*
Il Falconiere
Fat Boy's*
Fats
Formula Veneta*
The Gate*
El Gaucho*
Geale's
The Havelock Tavern
The Imperial Arms
Kalamaras, Micro
Khan's of Kensington

INDEXES

The Ladbroke Arms*
Latymers
Lisboa Patisserie
Lou Pescadou
Luigi's Delicatessen
Made in Italy
Manzara
Mediterraneo
Mona Lisa
Osteria Basilico
Palatino
Pâtisserie Valerie: SW3
Paulo's
PizzaExpress: The Pheasantry, 150-152 King's Road SW3*; SW6, W14, W2, W4, W8
The Polish Club*
Pret A Manger: SW3
Pucci Pizza
Raoul's Café
The Red Pepper
Riccardo's
Le Shop
Silks & Spice: all branches
Southeast
Spago
Sporting Page
Stick & Bowl
Stock Pot: Basil St SW3
The Terrace
Thai Bistro
Tom's*
Vingt-Quatre
The Westbourne*
Windsor Castle*
Wine Gallery*
Yas

North

Ask! Pizza: all north branches
Bar Gansa
Café Mozart*
Centuria
The Chapel
Crown & Goose
Daphne*
Ed's Easy Diner: NW3
Florians
The Fox Reformed*
Frederick's*
Greek Valley
Kavanagh's
Lansdowne
Lemonia
The Little Bay
Mango Room
Nontas*
Odette's
Pasha
La Piragua
PizzaExpress: Parkway NW1, Haverstock Hill NW3, NW8
La Porchetta Pizzeria
Le Sacré-Coeur
Sarcan
Silks & Spice: all branches
Soulard
The Vine*

South

Arancia
Babur Brasserie
Battersea Rickshaw
Boiled Egg*
Buchan's
Buona Sera
The Butlers Wharf Chophouse*
Café de la Place*
Café Portugal
Cantinetto Venegazzú*
don Fernando's
Ghillies: SW17*
Gourmet Pizza Co.: SE1*
Heather's*
The Honest Cabbage
Hornimans*
La Lanterna
The Lavender: SW11
Newton's
Ost. Antica Bologna
Phoenix
Pizza Metro
PizzaExpress: Chapter Ho, Montague Cl SE1, SW15, SW4
Le Pont de la Tour Bar & Grill*
Ransome's Dock*
The Ship*
The Stable
The Sun & Doves*
Le Versailles
White Cross Hotel*
Zed

East

Aquarium*
Arkansas Café
Barcelona Tapas: EC3
Café Indiya
Carnevale*
The Eagle
Frocks*
Futures*
Gourmet Pizza Co.: E14
Lunch*
Moshi Moshi Sushi: EC4
The Place Below*
Pret A Manger: EC1

INDEXES

Pre/Post theatre
(evening opening times are given; * open all day)

Central
Alfred *(6)*
Andrew Edmunds *(6)*
Blues *(6)*
Boudin Blanc *(6)*
Café Bohème*
Café du Jardin *(5.30)*
Café Sofra: *all branches**
Chiang Mai *(6)*
Chuen Cheng Ku*
Ed's Easy Diner: *Moor St W1**
Gopal's of Soho *(6)*
Gordon's Wine Bar*
Hamine*
Harbour City*
Ikkyu: *WC2**
The Lexington *(6)*
Manzi's *(5.30, 6 upstairs)*
Melati*
Mon Plaisir *(6)*
Mr Kong*
New World*
PizzaExpress: *Baker St W1, Bruton Pl W1, Charlotte St W1, Greek St W1, Dean St W1, Barrett St W1, Wardour St W1, WC1, Bow St WC2**
Pizzeria Condotti*
Pollo*
Poons*
Poons, Lisle Street*
Pret A Manger: *WC2**
Ristorante Italiano *(5.30)*
Shampers*
Sofra: *Shepherd St W1, St Christopher's Pl W1, both WC2**
Sri Siam *(6)*
Stock Pot: *SW1, Old Compton St W1**
Tokyo Diner*
Wagamama: *WC1**
Wolfe's*
Wong Kei*

North
Frederick's *(6)*

East
Alba *(6)*
Café Sofra: *all branches**

Private rooms
*(for the most comprehensive listing of venues for functions – from palaces to pubs – see **Harden's London Party Guide**, available in all good bookshops)*
* *particularly recommended*

Central
Alfred *(16)*
Aurora *(20)*
Blue Jade *(40)*
Blues *(40)*
Boudin Blanc *(35)*
Café du Jardin *(55)*
Café Latino *(20,40,16)*
Café Sofra: *Old Compton St W1, Wigmore St W1 (20)*
Chiang Mai *(25)*
China City *(20,30,50)*
Chuen Cheng Ku *(20-300)*
Efes Kebab House: *Great Titchfield St W1 (45)*
L'Estaminet *(22)*
Golden Dragon *(40)*
Harbour City *(40,60,70)*
Hunan *(20)*
Ikkyu: *W1 (10)*
Ishbilia *(8)*
Jenny Lo's *(20)*
Joy King Lau *(60)*
Little Havana *(150/60/40)*
Malabar Junction *(40)*
The Marquis *(25,30)**
Matsuri *(18)*
Mediterranean Café *(4)*
Mirabelle *(40, 40)**
Momo *(60)*
Mon Plaisir *(28)*
New World *(200)*
Nine Golden Square *(28–40)*
Pâtisserie Valerie: *RIBA Centre, 66 Portland Pl W1 (20)*
Pizza On The Park *(100)*
PizzaExpress: *Charlotte St W1 (40); Bruton Pl W1, Dean St W1, Barrett St W1 (70)*
Pizzeria Condotti *(40)*
Poons *(20)*
La Poule au Pot *(15)*
Purple Sage *(30)**
Ragam *(20)*
Rasa: *W1 (45)*
Ristorante Italiano *(25,40)*
Roussillon *(25)*
Royal China: *W1 (12)*
Shampers *(45)*
Silks & Spice: *W1 (60)*
Sofra: *Shepherd Mkt W1 (20); Tavistock St WC2 (90)*
Soho Spice *(30)*
Sri Siam *(32 & 26)*

INDEXES

Star Café *(35)*
Townhouse Brasserie *(38)*
Uno *(16)*
Veeraswamy *(36)*

West
Adams Café *(24)*
Anonimato *(20)*
Bar Japan *(6)*
Blah! Blah! Blah! *(30)*
Bluebird *(24)**
Blythe Road *(22)*
Brass. du Marché *(35)*
Brilliant *(80)*
Chelsea Ram *(12)*
Chutney Mary *(40)*
Coopers Arms *(40)*
Costa's Grill *(20)*
Coyote Café *(15)*
The Crescent *(70)*
The Cross Keys *(40)*
Daquise *(28)*
Emile's: *SW6 (42)*
Il Falconiere *(30)*
Fats *(30)*
Formula Veneta *(30)*
Front Page *(25)*
Good Earth *(40)*
Launceston Place *(30,14)*
Lou Pescadou *(45)*
Madhu's Brilliant *(52)*
Malabar *(24)*
Paulo's *(20)*
PizzaExpress: *Beauchamp Pl SW3 (20); SW6 (30); The Pheasantry, 150-152 King's Road SW3 (65)*
The Polish Club *(40)*
Pucci Pizza *(50)*
Raoul's Café *(18)*
Riccardo's *(10)*
Royal China: *W2 (15,20)*
S&P: *Fulham Rd SW3 (16)*
Le Shop *(40)*
Spago *(50)*
Standard Tandoori *(55)*
Stick & Bowl *(20)*
Wine Gallery *(40,18)*
Wódka *(30)*

North
Afghan Kitchen *(30)*
The Chapel *(30)*
Crown & Goose *(20)*
Daphne *(50)*
Diwana Bhel-Poori House *(40)*
Don Pepe *(25)*
La Finca: *N1 (150)*
Florians *(23,50)*
Frederick's *(30,20)*
Geeta *(10-30)*
Great Nepalese *(32)*
Greek Valley *(30)*
Gresslin's *(16)*
Lansdowne *(32)*
Lemonia *(40)*
The Little Bay *(15)*
Mango Room *(30)*
Odette's *(8.30)**
PizzaExpress: *N1, Kentish Town Road NW1 (30); Heath St NW3, NW8 (40)*
Sarcan *(40)*
Soulard *(16)*
The Vegetarian Cottage *(20)*
Weng Wah House *(80)*
ZeNW3 *(30)*

South
Alma *(70)*
The Apprentice *(55)*
Beyoglu *(35)*
Buchan's *(50-60)*
Emile's: *SW15 (45,30)*
Ghillies: *SW17 (25)*
La Lanterna *(56)*
Monsieur Max *(10,20)*
The North Pole *(30)*
Le P'tit Normand *(20)*
Phoenix *(30)*
PizzaExpress: *SW15 (30); Chapter Ho, Montague Cl SE1 (80)*
Scoffers *(12)*
The Ship *(14-20)*
Shree Krishna *(80)*
Zed *(60)*

East
Alba *(30)*
Aquarium *(130)*
Arkansas Café *(50)*
Café Spice Namaste *(35)*
Fox & Anchor *(8,7,24)*
Frocks *(26)*
Hope & Sir Loin *(30,25)*
Leadenhall Tapas Bar *(80)*
Lunch *(20)*
PizzaExpress: *EC2 (200)*
St John *(18)*
Shanghai *(60, 40)*

INDEXES

Vegetarian

★★
Chiang Mai *(W1)*
The Gate *(W6)*
Kastoori *(SW17)*
Rasa *(N16, W1)*
Shree Krishna *(SW17)*

🅰★
Food for Thought *(WC2)*
Malabar Junction *(WC1)*

★
Blah! Blah! Blah! *(W12)*
Carnevale *(EC1)*
Chutneys *(NW1)*
Diwana Bhel-Poori House *(NW1)*
Futures *(EC3)*
Geeta *(NW6)*
Heather's *(SE8)*
Manna *(NW3)*
Mildreds *(W1)*
Museum St Café *(WC1)*
Neal's Yard Dining Rooms *(WC2)*
The Place Below *(EC2)*
Ragam *(W1)*
Vijay *(NW6)*
Yum Yum *(N16)*

-
Futures *(EC2)*
India Club *(WC2)*
Mandeer *(WC1)*
Rani *(N3)*
The Vegetarian Cottage *(NW3)*
Woodlands *(SW1, W1)*

CUISINE INDEXES

CUISINES – EUROPE

British, Modern

Ⓐ★★
Launceston Place (W8)
Odette's (NW1)
Ransome's Dock (SW11)
The Stepping Stone (SW8)
The Terrace (W8)

★★
The Apprentice (SE1)
Chelsea Ram (SW10)
Chiswick (W4)
Gresslin's (NW3)
Nine Golden Square (W1)

Ⓐ★
Andrew Edmunds (W1)
Anglesea Arms (W6)
Aurora (W1)
Bank (WC2)
Bluebird (SW3)
Blues (W1)
Blythe Road (W14)
Café du Jardin (WC2)
Cantaloupe (EC2)
Coopers Arms (SW3)
Frederick's (N1)
Home (EC1)
The Lavender (SW11, SW9)
The Marquis (W1)
The Mason's Arms (SW8)
Scoffers (SW11)
The Sun & Doves (SE5)

★
Alfred (WC2)
Anonimato (W10)
The Chapel (NW1)
Crown & Goose (NW1)
Cucina (NW3)
Granita (N1)
The Havelock Tavern (W14)
Helter Skelter (SW9)
The Honest Cabbage (SE1)
Kavanagh's (N1)
The Ladbroke Arms (W11)
Mesclun (N16)
Le Metro (SW3)
Moxon's (SW4)
Museum St Café (WC1)
Nayab (SW6)
The North Pole (SE10)
Phoenix (SW15)
The Prince Bonaparte (W2)
Raoul's Café (W9)
St John (EC1)
Stone Mason's Arms (W6)
Vincent's (SW15)
The Vine (NW5)

Ⓐ
Buchan's (SW11)
The Crescent (SW3)
Dove (W6)
Frocks (E9)
Lansdowne (NW1)
Mango Room (NW1)
Mas Café (W11)
Patio (W12)
The Stable (SW13)
Vingt-Quatre (SW10)
The Westbourne (W2)
White Cross Hotel (TW9)

-
The Imperial Arms (SW6)
The Lexington (W1)
Soho Brewing
  Company (WC2)
Star Café (W1)
The Union Café (W1)

British, Traditional

★★
Fryer's Delight (WC1)
Seashell (NW1)
Toff's (N10)
Two Brothers (N3)

Ⓐ★
Ffiona's (W8)
Fox & Anchor (EC1)
Hope & Sir Loin (EC1)
Simpson's of Cornhill (EC3)

★
The Butlers Wharf Chop-
  house (SE1)
Costa's Fish (W8)
Fat Boy's (W4)
Geale's (W8)
Nautilus (NW6)
Seafresh (SW1)
Upper St Fish Shop (N1)

Ⓐ
Grenadier (SW1)
Reynier (EC3)
RK Stanleys (W1)
Windsor Castle (W8)

-
Brady's (SW18)
Star Café (W1)

Fish & seafood

★★
Chez Liline (N4)
Lou Pescadou (SW5)

CUISINES – EUROPE

Mandarin Kitchen *(W2)*

Ⓐ★
Bank *(WC2)*
Mediterraneo *(W11)*
Le Pont de la Tour Bar & Grill *(SE1)*

★
Ghillies *(SW17, SW6)*
Moxon's *(SW4)*
Polygon Bar & Grill *(SW4)*

Ⓐ
Aquarium *(E1)*
Manzi's *(WC2)*

-
Café Fish *(W1)*

French

Ⓐ★★
Mirabelle *(W1)*
Mon Plaisir *(WC2)*
La Poule au Pot *(SW1)*

★★
Lou Pescadou *(SW5)*
Le P'tit Normand *(SW18)*
Roussillon *(SW1)*

Ⓐ★
The Abingdon *(W8)*
Boudin Blanc *(W1)*
Brass. du Marché *(W10)*
Gastro *(SW4)*
Le Sacré-Coeur *(N1)*
Soulard *(N1)*

★
Café de la Place *(SW11)*
Emile's *(SW15, SW6)*
L'Estaminet *(WC2)*
Francofill *(SW7)*
Monsieur Max *(TW12)*
Townhouse Brasserie *(WC1)*
Le Versailles *(SW9)*

Ⓐ
Café Bohème *(W1)*
Randall & Aubin *(W1)*

-
Newton's *(SW4)*

Game

Ⓐ★
The Marquis *(W1)*

German

-
Café Mozart *(N6)*

Greek

★★
Beyoglu *(SW11)*

Ⓐ★
Costa's Grill *(W8)*
Lemonia *(NW1)*

★
Café O *(SW3)*
Daphne *(NW1)*
Kalamaras, Micro *(W2)*
Nontas *(NW1)*
Vrisaki *(N22)*

-
Greek Valley *(NW8)*
Halepi *(W2)*
Wine & Kebab *(SW10)*

Hungarian

-
Café Mozart *(N6)*

Italian

Ⓐ★★
Cibo *(W14)*

★★
Antipasto & Pasta *(SW11)*
Luigi's Delicatessen *(SW10)*
Pizzeria Franco *(SW9)*

Ⓐ★
Elistano *(SW3)*
Osteria Basilico *(W11)*
Pizzeria Castello *(SE1)*
La Porchetta Pizzeria *(N4)*
Purple Sage *(W1)*

★
Arancia *(SE16)*
Café 206 *(W11)*
Cantina Italia *(N1)*
Cantinetto Venegazzú *(SW11)*
Da Pierino *(SW7)*
La Delizia *(SW5)*
Il Falconiere *(SW7)*
Italian Kitchen *(WC2)*
Leonardo's *(SW10)*
Made in Italy *(SW3)*
Mona Lisa *(SW10)*
Oliveto *(SW1)*

CUISINES – EUROPE

Ost. Antica Bologna *(SW11)*
Palatino *(W4)*
Pollo *(W1)*
The Red Pepper *(W9)*
Riccardo's *(SW3)*
Spago *(SW7)*
La Spiga *(W1)*
La Spighetta *(W1)*
Uno *(SW1)*

🅰
Buona Sera *(SW11)*
Café Montpeliano *(SW3)*
Da Mario *(SW7)*
Florians *(N8)*
Formula Veneta *(SW10)*
Ristorante Italiano *(W1)*

-
Alba *(EC1)*
Bersagliera *(SW3)*
King's Road Café *(SW3)*
La Lanterna *(SE1)*

Mediterranean

🅰★
The Eagle *(EC1)*
Hujo's *(W1)*
Mediterraneo *(W11)*

★
Made in Italy *(SW3)*
Mediterranean Café *(W1)*

🅰
The Cross Keys *(SW3)*

-
Centuria *(N1)*
Newton's *(SW4)*

Polish

★
Wódka *(W8)*

🅰
The Polish Club *(SW7)*

-
Café Mozart *(N6)*
Daquise *(SW7)*
Zamoyski *(NW3)*

Portuguese

★
Café Portugal *(SW8)*

Steaks & grills

★★
Popeseye *(W14)*

🅰★
Fox & Anchor *(EC1)*
Hope & Sir Loin *(EC1)*
Le Pont de la Tour Bar & Grill *(SE1)*
Simpson's of Cornhill *(EC3)*

★
Arkansas Café *(E1)*
Café Coq *(WC2)*
Polygon Bar & Grill *(SW4)*
Wolfe's *(WC2)*

-
El Gaucho *(SW3)*

Spanish

🅰★
Bar Gansa *(NW1)*
Don Pepe *(NW8)*

★
Barcelona Tapas *(E1, EC3)*

🅰
don Fernando's *(TW9)*
La Finca *(N1, SE11)*
La Mancha *(SW15)*
Meson don Felipe *(SE1)*
Rebato's *(SW8)*
La Rueda *(SW4)*

-
Galicia *(W10)*
Goya *(SW1)*
Leadenhall Tapas Bar *(EC3)*

International

🅰★
Coopers Arms *(SW3)*

★
Chelsea Kitchen *(SW3)*
Heather's *(SE8)*
Stock Pot *(SW1, SW3, W1)*

🅰
Alphabet *(W1)*
Balans *(W1)*
Balans West *(SW5)*
Café Grove *(W11)*
Dove *(W6)*
The Fox Reformed *(N16)*
Front Page *(SW3)*
Gordon's Wine Bar *(WC2)*

CUISINES – 'SNACK' FOOD

The Little Bay (NW6)
Sarastro (WC2)
Shampers (W1)
The Ship (SW18)
Sporting Page (SW10)
Windsor Castle (W8)
Wine Gallery (SW10)

-
Alma (SW18)
Brahms (SW1)
Café Emm (W1)
Hodgson's Wine Bar (WC2)
Hornimans (SW4)
Lunch (EC1)
West End Kitchen (SW1)

Afternoon tea

🄰★
Aurora (W1)

-
Daquise (SW7)

Burgers, etc

★
Arkansas Café (E1)
Wolfe's (WC2)

🄰
Hard Rock Café (W1)
Sticky Fingers (W8)

-
Ed's Easy Diner (NW3, SW3, W1)

Fish & chips

★★
Faulkner's (E8)
Fryer's Delight (WC1)
Seashell (NW1)
Toff's (N10)
Two Brothers (N3)

★
Costa's Fish (W8)
Geale's (W8)
Nautilus (NW6)
Seafresh (SW1)
Upper St Fish Shop (N1)

-
Brady's (SW18)

Pizza

★★
Eco (SW4)

Pizza Metro (SW11)
Pizzeria Franco (SW9)

🄰★
Pizzeria Castello (SE1)
Pizzeria Condotti (W1)
La Porchetta Pizzeria (N4)
Pucci Pizza (SW3)

★
Cantina Italia (N1)
La Delizia (SW5)
Gourmet Pizza Co. (E14, SE1, W1)
Oliveto (SW1)
PizzaExpress (EC2, EC4, N1, N6, NW1, NW3, NW8, SE1, SW1, SW10, SW11, SW14, SW15, SW18, SW3, SW4, SW6, W1, W11, W14, W2, W4, W8, WC1, WC2)
The Red Pepper (W9)
Spago (SW7)
La Spiga (W1)

🄰
Buona Sera (SW11)
Da Mario (SW7)
Pizza On The Park (SW1)
Pizza Pomodoro (SW3)
Zed (SW2)

-
Ask! Pizza (EC1, N1, NW3, SW1, SW6, SW7, W1, W11, W2, W4, W8)

Sandwiches, cakes, etc

★★
Lisboa Patisserie (W10)

🄰★
Pâtisserie Valerie (SW3, W1, WC2)
Tom's (W10)
Troubadour (SW5)

★
Brick Lane Beigel Bake (E1)
Corney & Barrow (WC2)
Fileric (SW7)
Pret A Manger (EC1, EC2, EC4, N1, NW1, SW1, SW3, W1, W6, W8, WC1, WC2)

🄰
Bar Italia (W1)
Café Grove (W11)
Coins (W11)
Maison Bertaux (W1)
Seattle Coffee Co (SW1, W1, W8, WC2)
Le Shop (SW3)

-
Boiled Egg (SW11)
EAT (EC4, SW1, WC2)

CUISINES – AMERICAS/ AFRICA / MIDDLE EAST

King's Road Café *(SW3)*
Manzara *(W11)*

Vegetarian

★★
Chiang Mai *(W1)*
The Gate *(W6)*
Kastoori *(SW17)*
Rasa *(N16, W1)*
Shree Krishna *(SW17)*

A★
Food for Thought *(WC2)*
Malabar Junction *(WC1)*

★
Blah! Blah! Blah! *(W12)*
Carnevale *(EC1)*
Chutneys *(NW1)*
Diwana Bhel-Poori House *(NW1)*
Futures *(EC3)*
Geeta *(NW6)*
Heather's *(SE8)*
Manna *(NW3)*
Mildreds *(W1)*
Museum St Café *(WC1)*
Neal's Yard Dining Rooms *(WC2)*
The Place Below *(EC2)*
Ragam *(W1)*
Vijay *(NW6)*
Yum Yum *(N16)*

-
Futures *(EC2)*
India Club *(WC2)*
Mandeer *(WC1)*
Rani *(N3)*
The Vegetarian Cottage *(NW3)*
Woodlands *(SW1, W1)*

American

★
Arkansas Café *(E1)*

Brazilian

A★
Paulo's *(W6)*

Cajun/creole

-
Fats *(W9)*

Mexican/TexMex

-
Coyote Café *(W4)*
La Perla *(WC2)*

South American

A★
La Piragua *(N1)*

A
Café Latino *(W1)*
Little Havana *(WC2)*

-
El Gaucho *(SW3)*
Havana *(W1)*

Afro-Caribbean

★
Calabash *(WC2)*
Smokey Joe's *(SW18)*

A
Mango Room *(NW1)*

-
Fats *(W9)*

North African

★★
Laurent *(NW2)*

A★
Momo *(W1)*
Pasha *(SW7)*

★
Adams Café *(W12)*

Sudanese

A★
Mandola *(W11)*

Tunisian

★★
Laurent *(NW2)*

★
Adams Café *(W12)*

Egyptian

★
Ali Baba *(NW1)*

CUISINES – MIDDLE EAST / ASIA

Kosher

★
Nautilus (NW6)

Lebanese

★★
Ranoush (W2)

★
Beirut Express (W2)
Maroush (SW3, W1, W2)

-
Ishbilia (SW1)

Persian

★★
Alounak (W14)

-
Isfehan (W2)
Yas (W14)

Turkish

★★
Beyoglu (SW11)

🅐★
Iznik (N5)

★
Pasha (N1)
Sarcan (N1)

-
Café Sofra (EC4, W1, WC1, WC2)
Efes Kebab House (W1)
Manzara (W11)
Sofra (W1, WC2)

Afghani

★
Afghan Kitchen (N1)

Burmese

★
Mandalay (W2)

Chinese

★★
Hunan (SW1)
Mandarin Kitchen (W2)
Royal China (W1)
Royal China (W2)

🅐★
Good Earth (SW3)
Gung-Ho (NW6)
ZeNW3 (NW3)

★
Golden Dragon (W1)
Joy King Lau (W1)
Mayflower (W1)
Mr Kong (WC2)
Poons (WC2)
Poons, Lisle Street (WC2)
Shanghai (E8)
Stick & Bowl (W8)
Weng Wah House (NW3)
Wong Kei (W1)

-
China City (WC2)
Chuen Cheng Ku (W1)
Harbour City (W1)
Jenny Lo's (SW1)
New World (W1)
The Vegetarian
  Cottage (NW3)

Chinese, Dim sum

★★
Royal China (W1)
Royal China (W2)

★
Golden Dragon (W1)
Joy King Lau (W1)
Shanghai (E8)

-
Chuen Cheng Ku (W1)
Harbour City (W1)
New World (W1)

Indian

★★
Babur Brasserie (SE23)
Brilliant (UB2)
Kastoori (SW17)
Lahore Kebab House (E1)
Ma Goa (SW15)
Rasa (N16, W1)
Shree Krishna (SW17)
Soho Spice (W1)

🅐★
Anglo Asian Tandoori (N16)
Chutney Mary (SW10)
Malabar Junction (WC1)
Veeraswamy (W1)

CUISINES – ASIA

★
Anarkali *(W6)*
Café Indiya *(E1)*
Café Spice Namaste *(E1)*
Chutneys *(NW1)*
Diwana Bhel-Poori House *(NW1)*
Geeta *(NW6)*
Gopal's of Soho *(W1)*
Great Nepalese *(NW1)*
Indian Ocean *(SW17)*
Khan's *(W2)*
Khan's of Kensington *(SW7)*
Madhu's Brilliant *(UB1)*
Malabar *(W8)*
Nayab *(SW6)*
Noor Jahan *(SW5)*
Ragam *(W1)*
Standard Tandoori *(W2)*
Tandoori Lane *(SW6)*
Vijay *(NW6)*

-
Battersea Rickshaw *(SW11)*
India Club *(WC2)*
Mandeer *(WC1)*
Rani *(N3)*
Rupee Room *(EC2)*
Woodlands *(SW1, W1)*

Indian, Southern

★★
Kastoori *(SW17)*
Rasa *(N16)*
Shree Krishna *(SW17)*

𝔸★
Malabar Junction *(WC1)*

★
Chutneys *(NW1)*
Diwana Bhel-Poori House *(NW1)*
Geeta *(NW6)*
Ragam *(W1)*
Vijay *(NW6)*

-
India Club *(WC2)*
Mandeer *(WC1)*
Rani *(N3)*
Woodlands *(SW1, W1)*

Indonesian

★
Melati *(W1)*

Japanese

★★
Inaho *(W2)*

★
Bu San *(N7)*
Café Japan *(NW11)*
Hamine *(W1)*
Ikkyu *(W1, WC2)*
Kulu Kulu *(W1)*
Matsuri *(SW1)*
Moshi Moshi Sushi *(EC2, EC4)*
Noto *(EC2, EC4)*
Sushi-Say *(NW2)*
Tokyo Diner *(WC2)*
Wagamama *(W1, WC1)*
Yoshino *(W1)*

𝔸
Satsuma *(W1)*
Yo! Sushi *(W1)*

-
Bar Japan *(SW5)*
Sushi Wong *(W8)*

Korean

★
Bu San *(N7)*

Malaysian

★
Café Spice Namaste *(E1)*
Melati *(W1)*

Misc oriental

★
Southeast *(W9)*

𝔸
East One *(EC1)*

Thai

★★
Chiang Mai *(W1)*
Topsy-Tasty *(W4)*

𝔸★
Ben's Thai *(W9)*
Churchill *(W8)*

★
Bangkok *(SW7)*
Bedlington Café *(W4)*
Esarn Kheaw *(W12)*
Fat Boy's *(W4)*

CUISINES – ASIA

Latymers *(W6)*
Noho *(W1)*
The Old School Thai *(SW11)*
The Pepper Tree *(SW4)*
Phuket *(SW11)*
S&P Patara *(SW3)*
Sabai Sabai *(W6)*
Sri Siam *(W1)*
Tawana *(W2)*
Thai Bistro *(W4)*
Thai Break *(W8)*
Thai Pot *(WC2)*
Yum Yum *(N16)*

-
Blue Jade *(SW1)*
Krungtap *(SW10)*
Manorom *(WC2)*
Newton's *(SW4)*
The Papaya Tree *(W8)*
Silks & Spice *(NW1, NW8, W1, W4)*
Thai Pot Express *(WC2)*

Tibetan

-
Tibetan Restaurant *(WC2)*

AREA OVERVIEWS

Where the ratings for a restaurant appear in brackets, eg (𝔸★), you can usually keep expenditure within our £20-a-head budget only at certain times of the day, or by sticking to a particular menu. Eating at other times or from the à la carte menu may be much more expensive.

AREA OVERVIEWS

CENTRAL

Soho, Covent Garden & Bloomsbury
(Parts of W1, all WC2 and WC1)

£20+			
	Bank	*British, Modern*	(𝔸★)
	Café Bohème	*French*	(𝔸)
	Sarastro	*International*	(𝔸)
	Chiang Mai	*Thai*	★★

£15+			
	Nine Golden Square	*British, Modern*	(★★)
	Andrew Edmunds	"	𝔸★
	Aurora	"	𝔸★
	Blues	"	(𝔸★)
	Café du Jardin	"	(𝔸★)
	Alfred	"	(★)
	Corney & Barrow	"	(★)
	Titanic	"	(★)
	Soho Brewing Company	"	-
	The Lexington	"	(-)
	Manzi's	*Fish & seafood*	(𝔸)
	L'Estaminet	*French*	(★)
	Townhouse Brasserie	"	(★)
	Randall & Aubin	"	(𝔸)
	Italian Kitchen	*Italian*	★
	Hujo's	*Mediterranean*	𝔸★
	Alphabet	*International*	𝔸
	Balans	"	𝔸
	Shampers	"	𝔸
	Café Emm	"	-
	Hodgson's Wine Bar	"	-
	Wolfe's	*Burgers, etc*	★
	La Spiga	*Pizza*	★
	Museum St Café	*Vegetarian*	★
	La Perla	*Mexican/TexMex*	-
	Café Latino	*South American*	𝔸
	Little Havana	"	(𝔸)
	Sofra	*Turkish*	-
	Golden Dragon	*Chinese*	★
	Mayflower	"	★
	China City	"	-
	Chuen Cheng Ku	"	-
	Harbour City	"	-
	Soho Spice	*Indian*	★★
	Malabar Junction	"	𝔸★
	Gopal's of Soho	"	★
	Ikkyu	*Japanese*	★
	Satsuma	"	𝔸
	Yo! Sushi	"	𝔸
	Melati	*Malaysian*	★
	Thai Pot	*Thai*	★

AREA OVERVIEWS

	Sri Siam	"	(★)
	Manorom	"	-
	Thai Pot Express	"	(-)
£10+	Star Café	British, Modern	-
	Mon Plaisir	French	(𝔸★★)
	Mediterranean Café	Mediterranean	★
	Café Coq	Steaks & grills	★
	Gordon's Wine Bar	International	𝔸
	Ed's Easy Diner	Burgers, etc	-
	PizzaExpress	Pizza	★
	Pâtisserie Valerie	Sandwiches, cakes, etc	𝔸★
	Food for Thought	Vegetarian	𝔸★
	Mildreds	"	★
	Neal's Yard Dining Rooms	"	★
	Calabash	Afro-Caribbean	★
	Joy King Lau	Chinese	★
	Mr Kong	"	★
	Poons	"	★
	Poons, Lisle Street	"	★
	Wong Kei	"	★
	New World	"	-
	India Club	Indian	-
	Hamine	Japanese	★
	Kulu Kulu	"	★
	Tokyo Diner	"	★
	Wagamama	"	★
	Tibetan Restaurant	Tibetan	-
£5+	Pollo	Italian	★
	Stock Pot	International	★
	Fryer's Delight	Fish & chips	★★
	Pret A Manger	Sandwiches, cakes, etc	★
	Bar Italia	"	𝔸
	Maison Bertaux	"	𝔸
	Seattle Coffee Co	"	𝔸
	EAT	"	-
	Café Sofra	Turkish	-

Mayfair & St James's
(Parts of W1 and SW1)

£20+	Mirabelle	French	(𝔸★★)
£15+	The Marquis	British, Modern	(𝔸★)
	Café Fish	Fish & seafood	(-)
	Ristorante Italiano	Italian	(𝔸)
	Hard Rock Café	Burgers, etc	𝔸
	Pizzeria Condotti	Pizza	𝔸★
	Gourmet Pizza Co.	"	★

AREA OVERVIEWS

	Ask! Pizza	"	-
	Havana	South American	-
	Momo	North African	(A★)
	Sofra	Turkish	-
	Rasa	Indian	★★
	Veeraswamy	"	(A★)
	Yoshino	Japanese	★
	Matsuri	"	(★)
£10+	Boudin Blanc	French	(A★)
	PizzaExpress	Pizza	★
	Woodlands	Indian	(-)
£5+	Stock Pot	International	★
	West End Kitchen	"	-
	Pret A Manger	Sandwiches, cakes, etc	★
	Seattle Coffee Co	"	A
	EAT	"	-
	Café Sofra	Turkish	-

Fitzrovia & Marylebone (Part of W1)

£15+	The Union Café	British, Modern	(-)
	RK Stanleys	British, Traditional	A
	Purple Sage	Italian	(A★)
	La Spighetta	"	★
	Ask! Pizza	Pizza	-
	Efes Kebab House	Turkish	-
	Sofra	"	
	Royal China	Chinese	★★
	Ikkyu	Japanese	★
	Noho	Thai	★
	Silks & Spice	"	-
£10+	PizzaExpress	Pizza	★
	Pâtisserie Valerie	Sandwiches, cakes, etc	A★
	Maroush	Lebanese	★
	Ragam	Indian	★
	Mandeer	"	-
	Woodlands	"	(-)
	Wagamama	Japanese	★
£5+	Stock Pot	International	★
	Pret A Manger	Sandwiches, cakes, etc	★
	Seattle Coffee Co	"	A
	Café Sofra	Turkish	-

AREA OVERVIEWS

**Belgravia, Victoria & Pimlico
(SW1, except St James's)**

£20+	Roussillon	French	(★★)
£15+	La Poule au Pot	"	(Ⓐ★★)
	Uno	Italian	★
	Goya	Spanish	-
	Oliveto	Pizza	(★)
	Ask! Pizza	"	-
	Ishbilia	Lebanese	(-)
	Hunan	Chinese	(★★)
	Blue Jade	Thai	-
£10+	Brahms	International	-
	Seafresh	Fish & chips	★
	PizzaExpress	Pizza	★
	Pizza On The Park	"	Ⓐ
	Jenny Lo's	Chinese	-
£5+	Grenadier	British, Traditional	Ⓐ
	Pret A Manger	Sandwiches, cakes, etc	★
	Seattle Coffee Co	"	Ⓐ

AREA OVERVIEWS

WEST

Chelsea, South Kensington, Kensington, Earl's Court & Fulham (SW3, SW5, SW6, SW7, SW10 & W8)

£20+	Launceston Place	British, Modern	(A★★)
	Bluebird	"	(A★)
	Wine & Kebab	Greek	(-)
£15+	The Terrace	British, Modern	(A★★)
	Chelsea Ram	"	★★
	Le Metro	"	★
	The Crescent	"	A
	Vingt-Quatre	"	A
	The Imperial Arms	"	-
	Ffiona's	British, Traditional	A★
	Ghillies	Fish & seafood	★
	Lou Pescadou	French	(★★)
	The Abingdon	"	(A★)
	Emile's	"	★
	Francofill	"	★
	Café O	Greek	(★)
	Elistano	Italian	A★
	Il Falconiere	"	★
	Riccardo's	"	★
	Leonardo's	"	(★)
	Café Montpeliano	"	A
	Da Mario	"	A
	Formula Veneta	"	(A)
	Bersagliera	"	-
	King's Road Café	"	-
	The Cross Keys	Mediterranean	(A)
	Wódka	Polish	(★)
	The Polish Club	"	A
	Coopers Arms	International	A★
	Balans West	"	A
	Front Page	"	A
	Sporting Page	"	A
	Wine Gallery	"	A
	Sticky Fingers	Burgers, etc	A
	Geale's	Fish & chips	★
	Pucci Pizza	Pizza	A★
	Pizza Pomodoro	"	A
	Ask! Pizza	"	-
	El Gaucho	South American	-
	Pasha	North African	(A★)
	Good Earth	Chinese	(A★)
	Chutney Mary	Indian	(A★)
	Malabar	"	★
	Nayab	"	★

AREA OVERVIEWS

	Noor Jahan	"	★
	Tandoori Lane	"	★
	Bar Japan	Japanese	-
	Sushi Wong	"	-
	Bangkok	Thai	★
	Thai Break	"	★
	S&P	"	(★)
	S&P Patara	"	(★)
£10+	Costa's Grill	Greek	Ⓐ★
	Luigi's Delicatessen	Italian	★★
	Da Pierino	"	★
	Made in Italy	"	★
	Spago	"	★
	Daquise	Polish	-
	Windsor Castle	International	Ⓐ
	Ed's Easy Diner	Burgers, etc	-
	Costa's Fish	Fish & chips	★
	La Delizia	Pizza	★
	PizzaExpress	"	★
	Pâtisserie Valerie	Sandwiches, cakes, etc	Ⓐ★
	Troubadour	"	Ⓐ★
	Le Shop	"	Ⓐ
	Maroush	Lebanese	(★)
	Khan's of Kensington	Indian	★
	Krungtap	Thai	-
	The Papaya Tree	"	-
£5+	Mona Lisa	Italian	★
	Chelsea Kitchen	International	★
	Stock Pot	"	★
	Fileric	Sandwiches, cakes, etc	★
	Pret A Manger	"	★
	Seattle Coffee Co	"	Ⓐ
	Stick & Bowl	Chinese	★
	Churchill	Thai	Ⓐ★

Notting Hill, Holland Park, Bayswater, North Kensington & Maida Vale (W2, W9, W10, W11)

£15+	The Ladbroke Arms	British, Modern	★
	The Prince Bonaparte	"	★
	Raoul's Café	"	★
	Anonimato	"	(★)
	The Westbourne	"	Ⓐ
	Mas Café	"	(Ⓐ)
	Brass. du Marché	French	(Ⓐ★)
	Kalamaras, Micro	Greek	★
	Halepi	"	-

AREA OVERVIEWS

	Osteria Basilico	Italian	(A★)
	Café 206	"	★
	The Red Pepper	"	★
	Mediterraneo	Mediterranean	A★
	Galicia	Spanish	-
	Ask! Pizza	Pizza	-
	Fats	Cajun/creole	
	Mandola	Sudanese	A★
	Beirut Express	Lebanese	★
	Isfehan	Persian	-
	Mandarin Kitchen	Chinese	★★
	Royal China	"	★★
	Khan's	Indian	★
	Inaho	Japanese	(★★)
	Southeast	Misc oriental	★
	Ben's Thai	Thai	A★
	Tawana	"	★
£10+	Café Grove	International	A
	PizzaExpress	Pizza	★
	Tom's	Sandwiches, cakes, etc	A★
	Coins	"	A
	Ranoush	Lebanese	★★
	Maroush	"	(★)
	Manzara	Turkish	-
	Mandalay	Burmese	★
	Standard Tandoori	Indian	★
£1+	Lisboa Patisserie	Sandwiches, cakes, etc	★★

Hammersmith, Shepherd's Bush Chiswick & Olympia (W4, W5, W6, W12, W14)

£15+	Chiswick	British, Modern	(★★)
	Anglesea Arms	"	A★
	Blythe Road	"	(A★)
	The Havelock Tavern	"	★
	Stone Mason's Arms	"	★
	Cibo	Italian	(A★★)
	Palatino	"	★
	Popeseye	Steaks & grills	★★
	Ask! Pizza	Pizza	-
	The Gate	Vegetarian	★★
	Blah! Blah! Blah!	"	★
	Paulo's	Brazilian	A★
	Coyote Café	Mexican/TexMex	-
	Adams Café	Tunisian	★
	Yas	Persian	-
	Anarkali	Indian	★

AREA OVERVIEWS

	Madhu's Brilliant	"	★
	Bedlington Café	*Thai*	★
	Esarn Kheaw	"	★
	Sabai Sabai	"	★
	Thai Bistro	"	★
	Silks & Spice	"	-
£10+	Dove	*British, Modern*	𝔸
	Patio	"	𝔸
	PizzaExpress	*Pizza*	★
	Alounak	*Persian*	★★
	Brilliant	*Indian*	★★
	Topsy-Tasty	*Thai*	★★
	Fat Boy's	"	★
	Latymers	"	★
£5+	Pret A Manger	*Sandwiches, cakes, etc*	★

AREA OVERVIEWS

NORTH

Hampstead, West Hampstead, St John's Wood, Regent's Park, Kilburn & Camden Town (NW postcodes)

£15+	Odette's	*British, Modern*	(𝔸★★)
	Gresslin's	"	(★★)
	The Chapel	"	★
	Cucina	"	(★)
	The Vine	"	(★)
	Lansdowne	"	𝔸
	Lemonia	*Greek*	𝔸★
	Daphne	"	★
	Greek Valley	"	-
	Zamoyski	*Polish*	-
	Seashell	*Fish & chips*	★★
	Ask! Pizza	*Pizza*	-
	Manna	*Vegetarian*	★
	Mango Room	*Afro-Caribbean*	𝔸
	Laurent	*Tunisian*	★★
	Gung-Ho	*Chinese*	(𝔸★)
	ZeNW3	"	(𝔸★)
	Weng Wah House	"	★
	The Vegetarian Cottage	"	-
	Café Japan	*Japanese*	★
	Sushi-Say	"	★
	Silks & Spice	*Thai*	-
£10+	Crown & Goose	*British, Modern*	★
	Nontas	*Greek*	★
	Bar Gansa	*Spanish*	𝔸★
	Don Pepe	"	𝔸★
	The Little Bay	*International*	𝔸
	Ed's Easy Diner	*Burgers, etc*	-
	Nautilus	*Fish & chips*	★
	PizzaExpress	*Pizza*	★
	Ali Baba	*Egyptian*	★
	Oriental City Food Ct	*Misc oriental*	★
	Chutneys	*Indian*	★
	Geeta	"	★
	Great Nepalese	"	★
	Vijay	"	★
£5+	Pret A Manger	*Sandwiches, cakes, etc*	★
	Diwana B.-Poori Hs	*Indian*	★

AREA OVERVIEWS

Islington, Highgate, Crouch End, Stoke Newington, Finsbury Park, Muswell Hill & Finchley (N postcodes)

£20+	Soulard	*French*	(𝔸★)
£15+	Frederick's	*British, Modern*	(𝔸★)
	Mesclun	"	★
	Granita	"	(★)
	Kavanagh's	"	(★)
	Chez Liline	*Fish & seafood*	(★★)
	Le Sacré-Coeur	*French*	𝔸★
	Vrisaki	*Greek*	★
	Cantina Italia	*Italian*	★
	Centuria	*Mediterranean*	-
	The Fox Reformed	*International*	𝔸
	Toff's	*Fish & chips*	★★
	Two Brothers	"	★★
	Upper St Fish Shop	"	★
	Ask! Pizza	*Pizza*	-
	Iznik	*Turkish*	𝔸★
	Pasha	"	★
	Rasa	*Indian*	★★
	Rani	"	-
	Yum Yum	*Thai*	★
£10+	Café Mozart	*German*	-
	La Porchetta Pizzeria	*Italian*	𝔸★
	Florians	"	(𝔸)
	La Finca	*Spanish*	𝔸
	PizzaExpress	*Pizza*	★
	La Piragua	*South American*	𝔸★
	Sarcan	*Turkish*	★
	Afghan Kitchen	*Afghani*	★
	Anglo Asian Tandoori	*Indian*	𝔸★
	Bu San	*Korean*	★
£5+	Pret A Manger	*Sandwiches, cakes, etc*	★

AREA OVERVIEWS

SOUTH

South Bank
(SE1)

£15+	The Apprentice	British, Modern	(★★)
	The Honest Cabbage	"	★
	The Butlers Wharf Chop-house	British, Traditional	(★)
	La Lanterna	Italian	-
	Le Pont de la Tour Bar & Grill	Steaks & grills	(𝔸★)
	Gourmet Pizza Co.	Pizza	★
£10+	Meson don Felipe	Spanish	𝔸
	Pizzeria Castello	Pizza	𝔸★
	PizzaExpress	"	★

Battersea, Clapham, Wandsworth, Barnes, Putney, Brixton & Lewisham
(All postcodes south of the river except SE1)

£15+	Ransome's Dock	British, Modern	(𝔸★★)
	The Stepping Stone	"	(𝔸★★)
	The Lavender	"	𝔸★
	The Mason's Arms	"	𝔸★
	Scoffers	"	𝔸★
	The Sun & Doves	"	𝔸★
	Helter Skelter	"	★
	The North Pole	"	(★)
	Phoenix	"	(★)
	Vincent's	"	(★)
	The Stable	"	𝔸
	Ghillies	Fish & seafood	★
	Moxon's	"	★
	Le P'tit Normand	French	(★★)
	Gastro	"	𝔸★
	Emile's	"	★
	Monsieur Max	"	(★)
	Le Versailles	"	(★)
	Newton's	"	(-)
	Antipasto & Pasta	Italian	★★
	Arancia	"	★
	Cantinetto Venegazzú	"	★
	Ost. Antica Bologna	"	★
	Buona Sera	"	𝔸
	Café Portugal	Portuguese	★
	Polygon Bar & Grill	Steaks & grills	(★)
	don Fernando's	Spanish	𝔸
	La Mancha	"	𝔸

AREA OVERVIEWS

	Name	Cuisine	Rating
	Rebato's	"	𝔸
	La Rueda	"	𝔸
	The Ship	International	𝔸
	Alma	"	-
	Hornimans	"	-
	Eco	Pizza	★★
	Pizza Metro	"	★★
	Zed	"	𝔸
	Smokey Joe's	Afro-Caribbean	★
	Beyoglu	Turkish	★★
	Babur Brasserie	Indian	★★
	Ma Goa	"	★★
	Indian Ocean	"	★
	Battersea Rickshaw	"	-
	The Old School Thai	Thai	★
	Phuket	"	★
£10+	White Cross Hotel	British, Modern	𝔸
	Buchan's	"	(𝔸)
	Café de la Place	French	★
	La Finca	Spanish	𝔸
	Brady's	Fish & chips	-
	Pizzeria Franco	Pizza	★★
	PizzaExpress	"	★
	Boiled Egg	Sandwiches, cakes, etc	-
	Heather's	Vegetarian	★
	Kastoori	Indian	★★
	Shree Krishna	"	★★
	The Pepper Tree	Thai	★

AREA OVERVIEWS

EAST

Smithfield & Farringdon
(EC1)

£15+	Home	*British, Modern*	(A★)
	Alba	*Italian*	(-)
	The Eagle	*Mediterranean*	A★
	Hope & Sir Loin	*Steaks & grills*	A★
	Ask! Pizza	*Pizza*	-
	Carnevale	*Vegetarian*	★
	East One	*Misc oriental*	A
£10+	St John	*British, Modern*	(★)
	Fox & Anchor	*British, Traditional*	A★
	Lunch	*International*	-
£5+	Pret A Manger	*Sandwiches, cakes, etc*	★

The City & East End
(All E and EC postcodes, except EC1)

£20+	Aquarium	*Fish & seafood*	(A)
	Café Spice Namaste	*Indian*	(★)
£15+	Frocks	*British, Modern*	(A)
	Simpson's of Cornhill	*British, Traditional*	A★
	Arkansas Café	*Steaks & grills*	★
	Gourmet Pizza Co.	*Pizza*	★
	Shanghai	*Chinese*	★
	Café Indiya	*Indian*	★
	Rupee Room	*"*	-
£10+	Cantaloupe	*British, Modern*	(A★)
	Reynier	*British, Traditional*	A
	Barcelona Tapas	*Spanish*	★
	Leadenhall Tapas Bar	*"*	-
	Faulkner's	*Fish & chips*	★★
	PizzaExpress	*Pizza*	★
	The Place Below	*Vegetarian*	★
	Lahore Kebab House	*Indian*	★★
	Moshi Moshi Sushi	*Japanese*	★
	Noto	*"*	★
£5+	Pret A Manger	*Sandwiches, cakes, etc*	★
	EAT	*"*	-
	Futures	*Vegetarian*	★
	Futures	*"*	-
	Café Sofra	*Turkish*	-
£1+	Brick Lane Beigel Bake	*Sandwiches, cakes, etc*	★

MAPS

MAP I – LONDON OVERVIEW

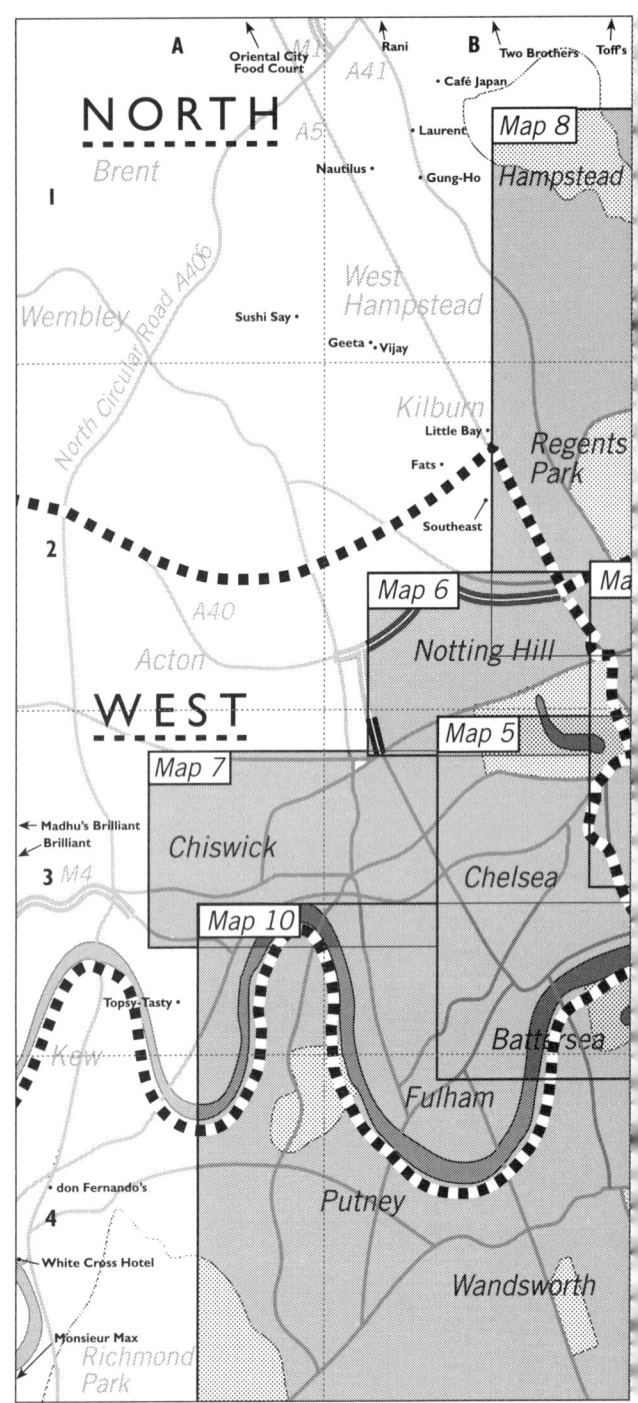

MAP 1 – LONDON OVERVIEW

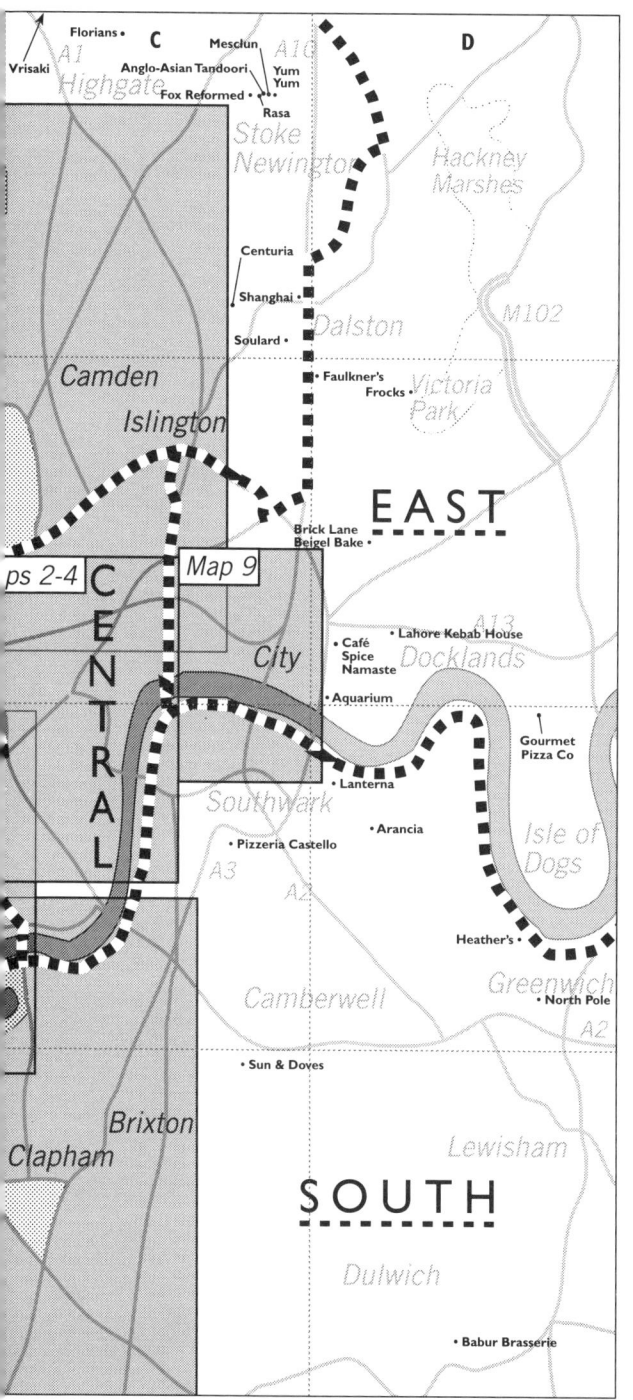

MAP 2 – WEST END OVERVIEW

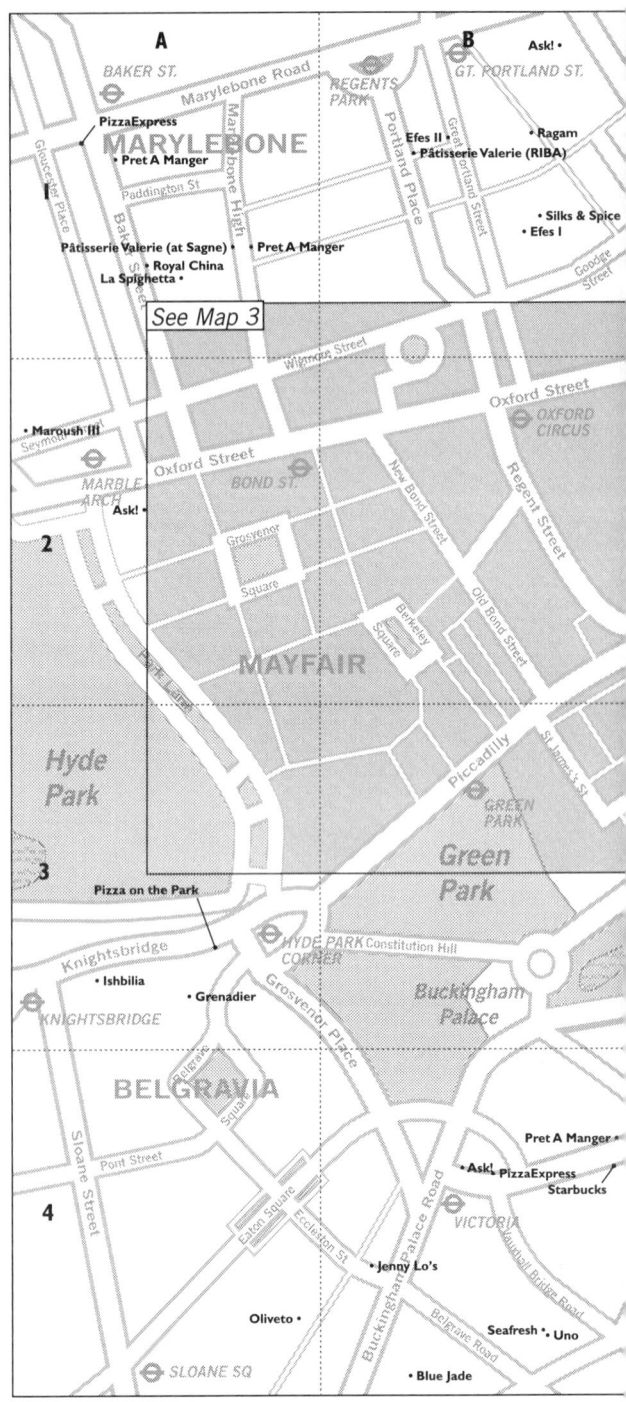

MAP 2 – WEST END OVERVIEW

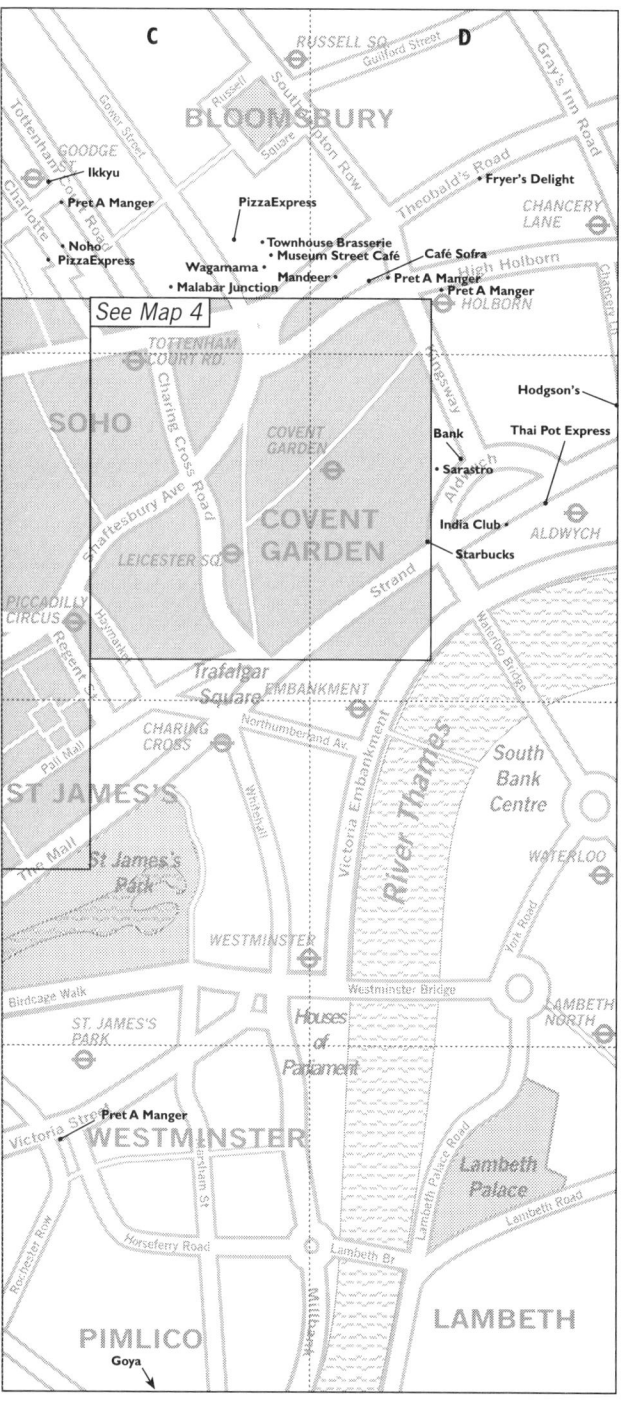

MAP 3 – MAYFAIR, ST JAMES'S & WEST SOHO

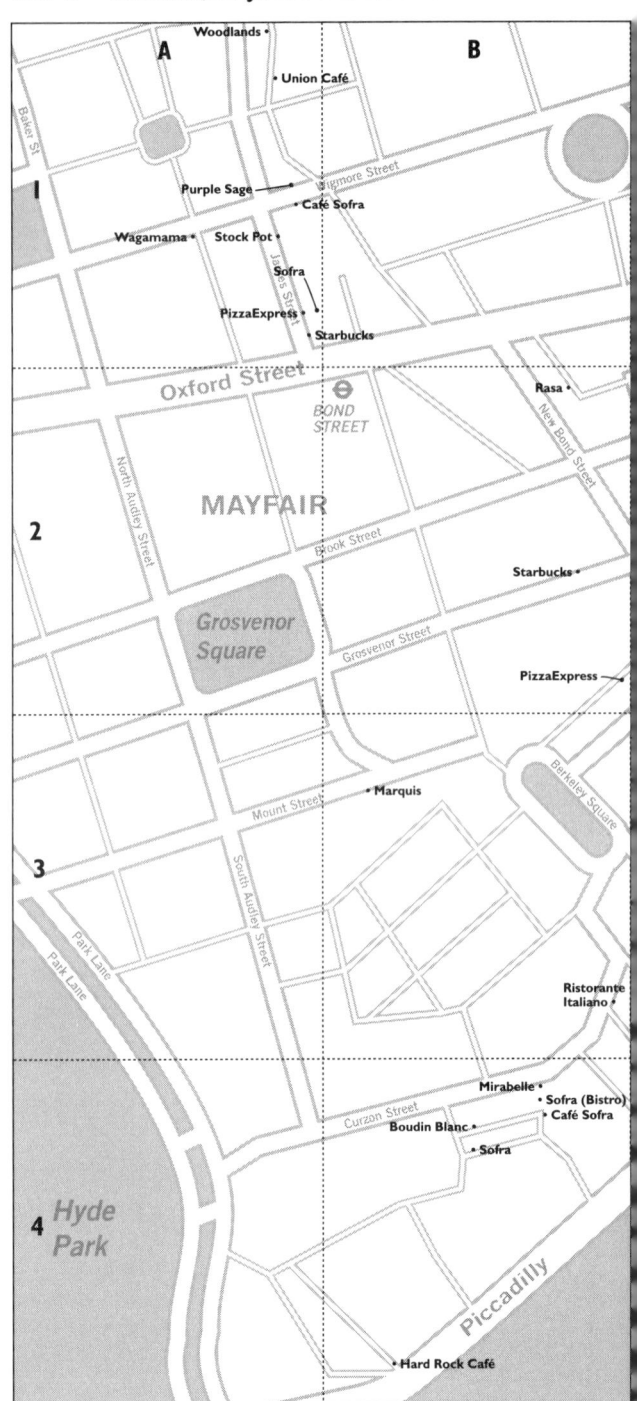

MAP 3 – MAYFAIR, ST JAMES'S & WEST SOHO

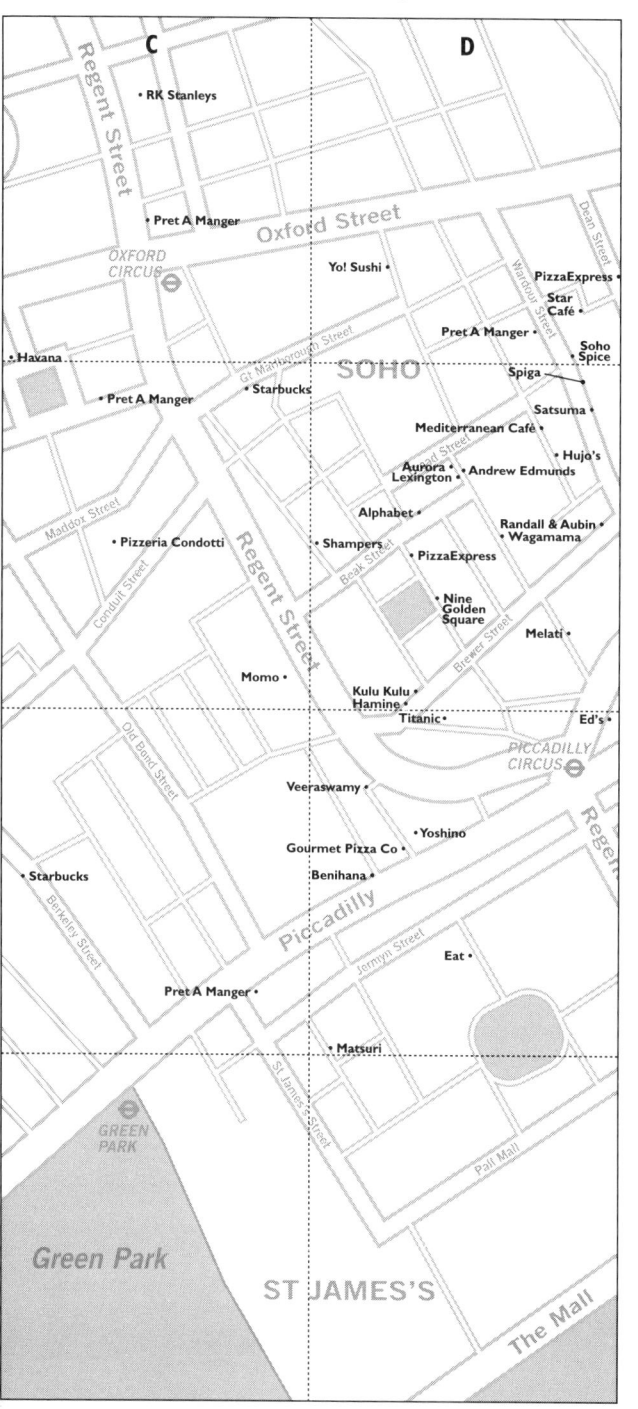

MAP 4 – EAST SOHO, CHINATOWN & COVENT GARDEN

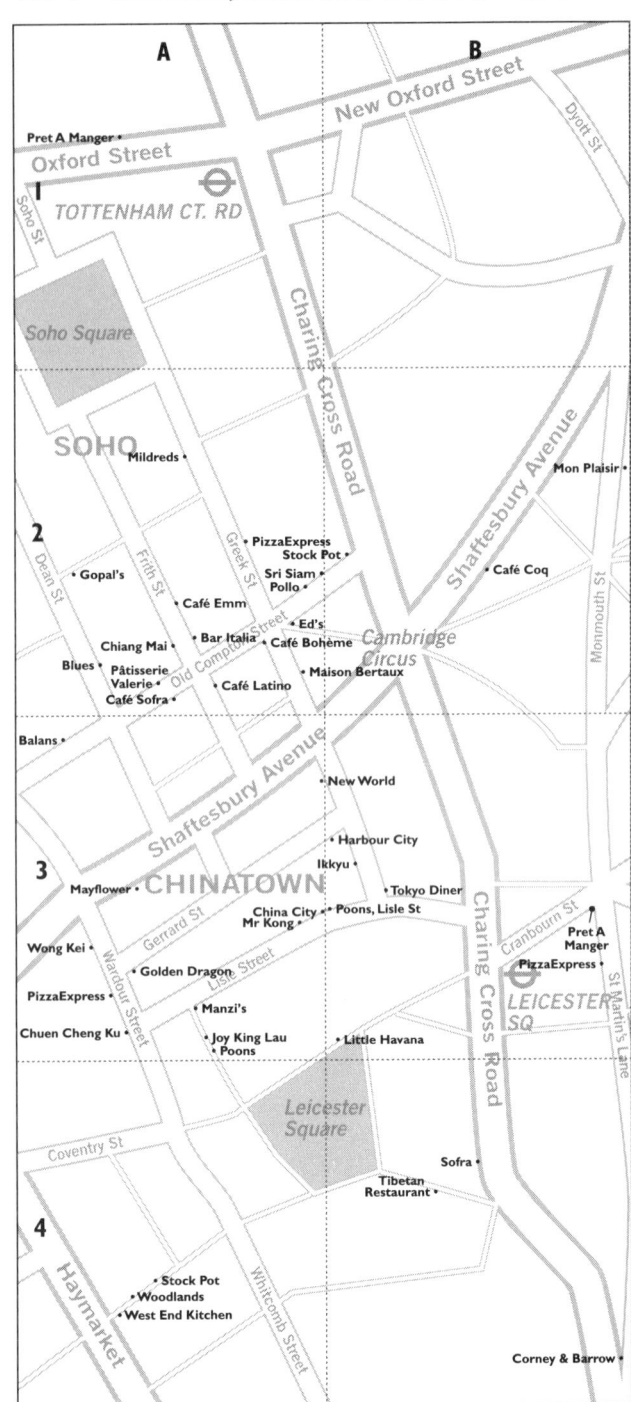

MAP 4 – EAST SOHO, CHINATOWN & COVENT GARDEN

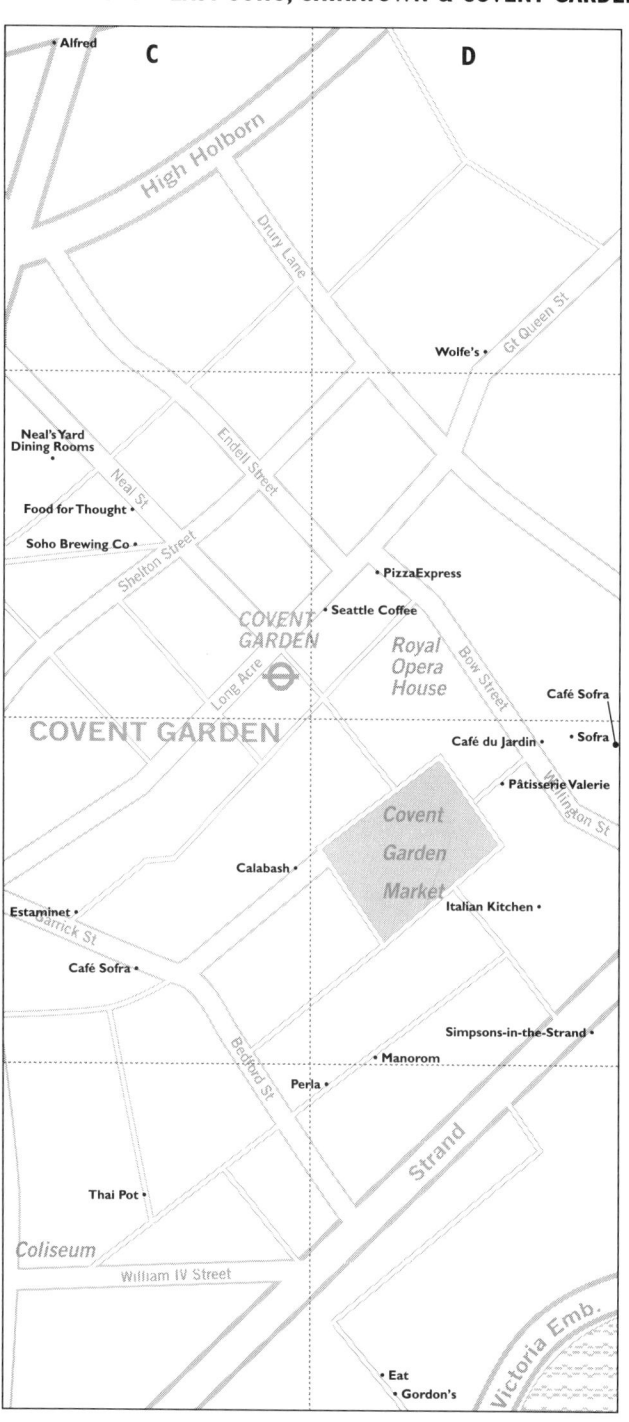

MAP 5 – KNIGHTSBRIDGE, CHELSEA & SOUTH KENSINGTON

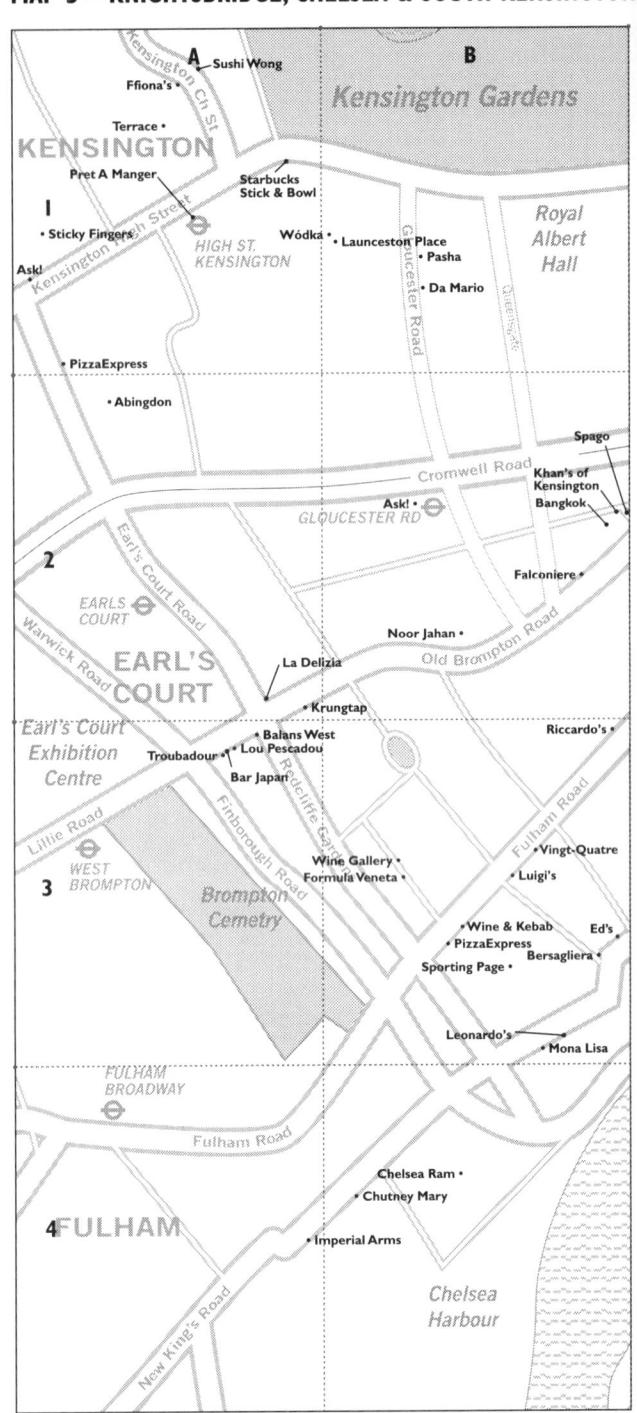

MAP 5 – KNIGHTSBRIDGE, CHELSEA & SOUTH KENSINGTON

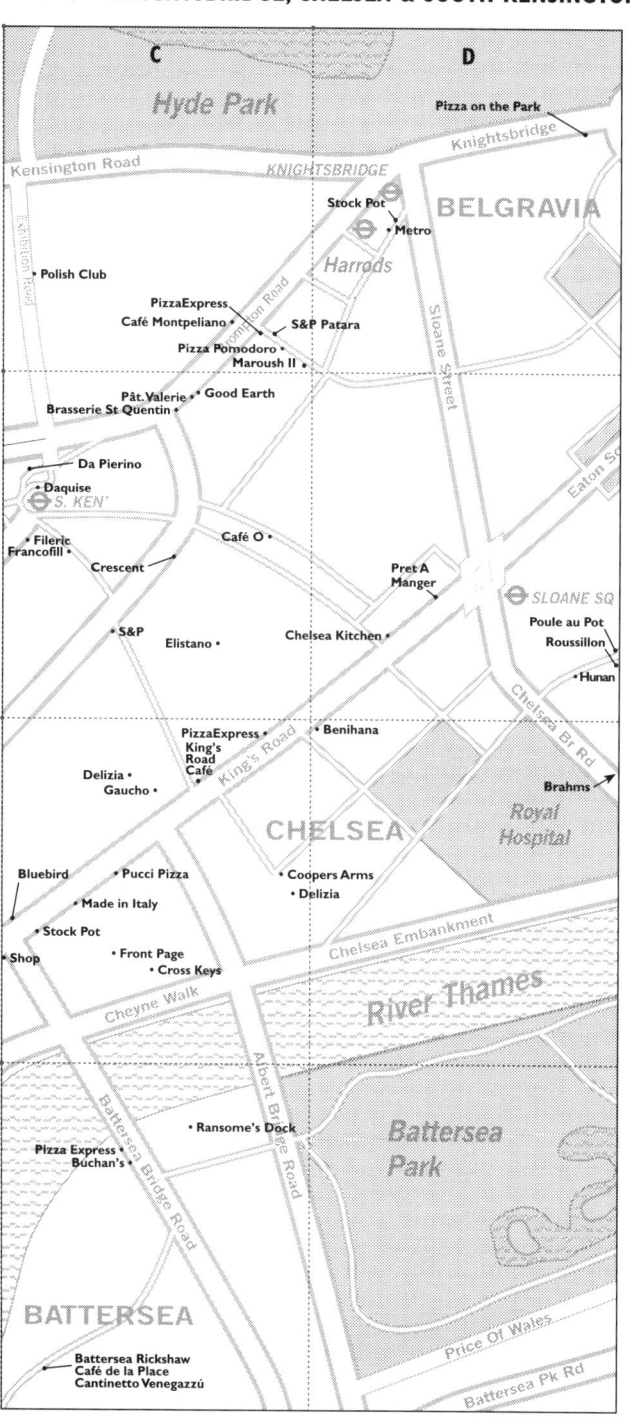

MAP 6 – NOTTING HILL & BAYSWATER

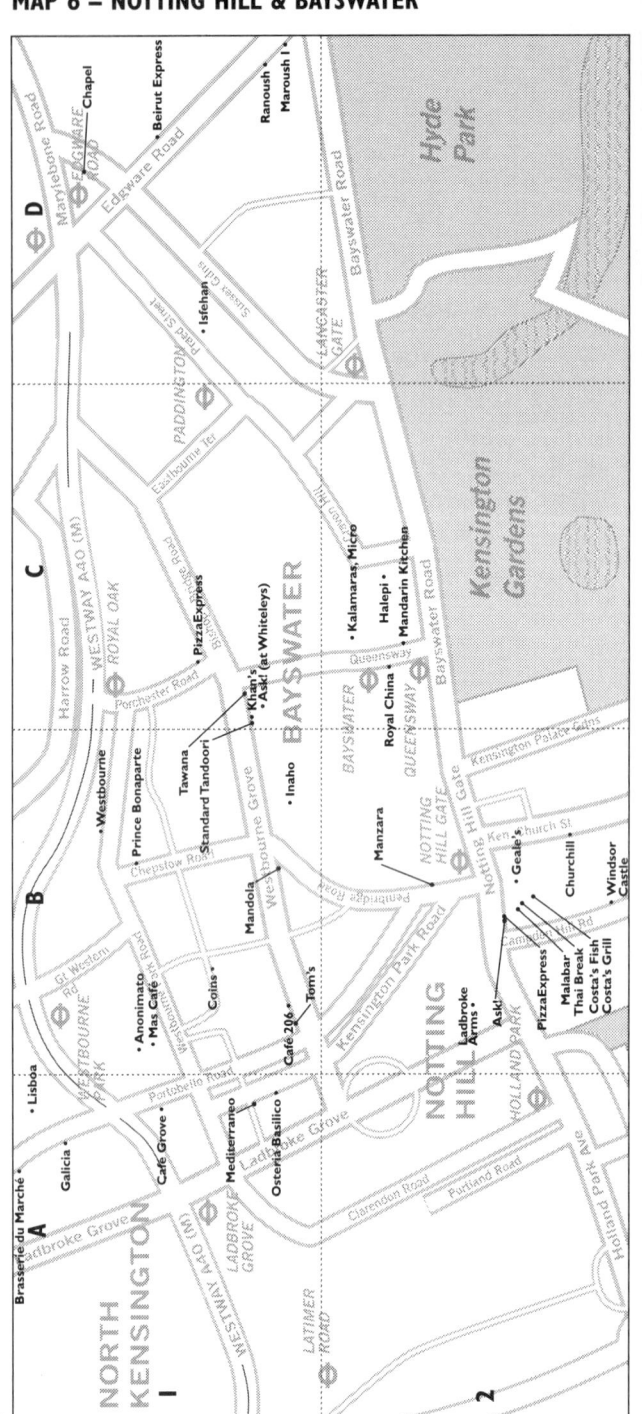

MAP 7 – HAMMERSMITH & CHISWICK

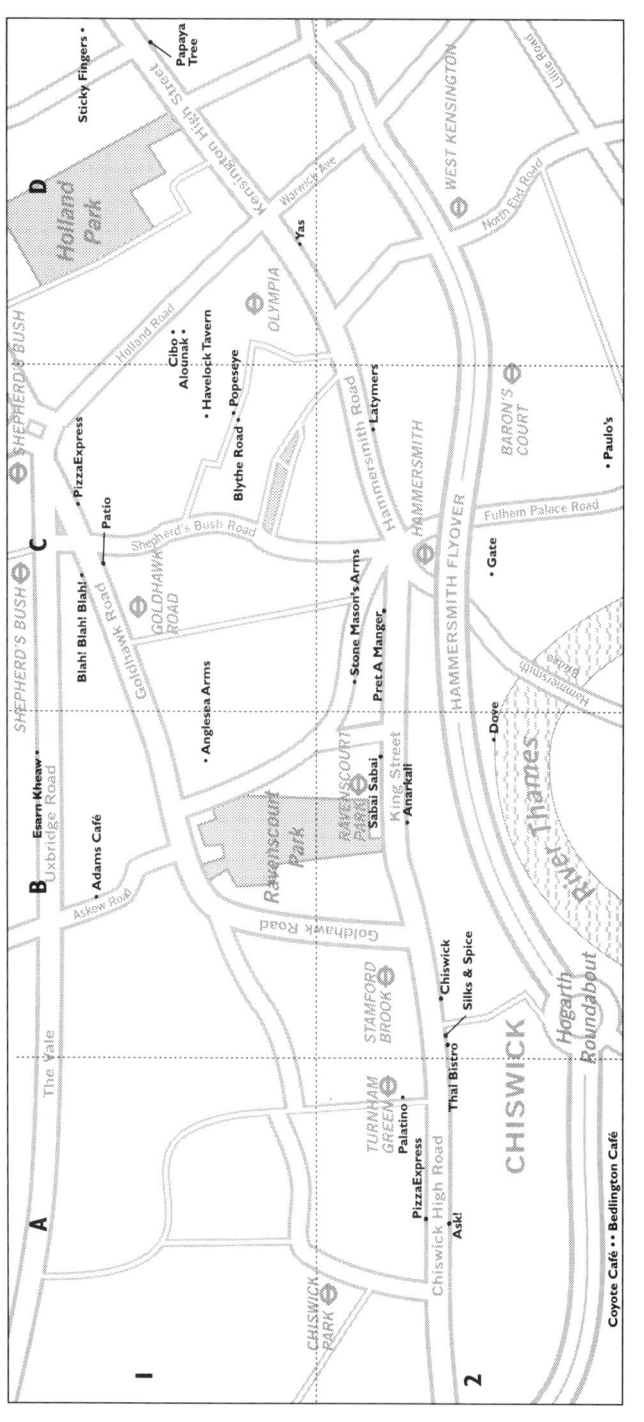

MAP 8 – HAMPSTEAD, CAMDEN TOWN & ISLINGTON

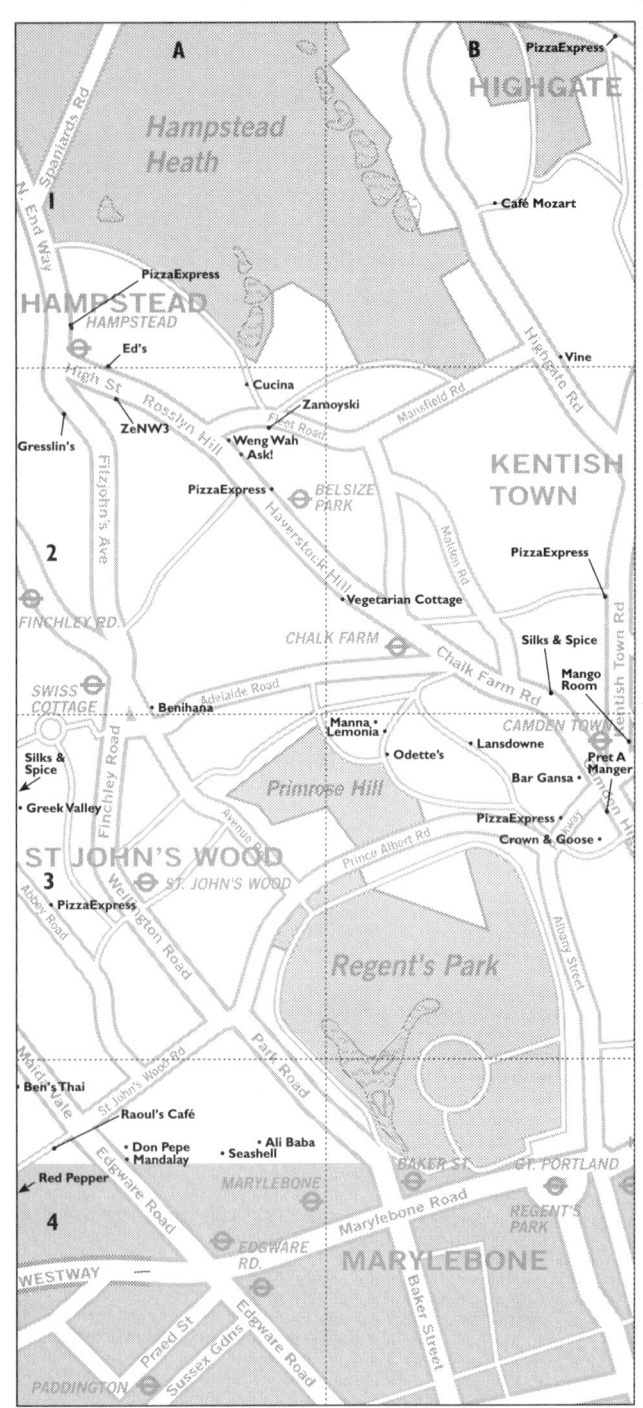

MAP 8 – HAMPSTEAD, CAMDEN TOWN & ISLINGTON

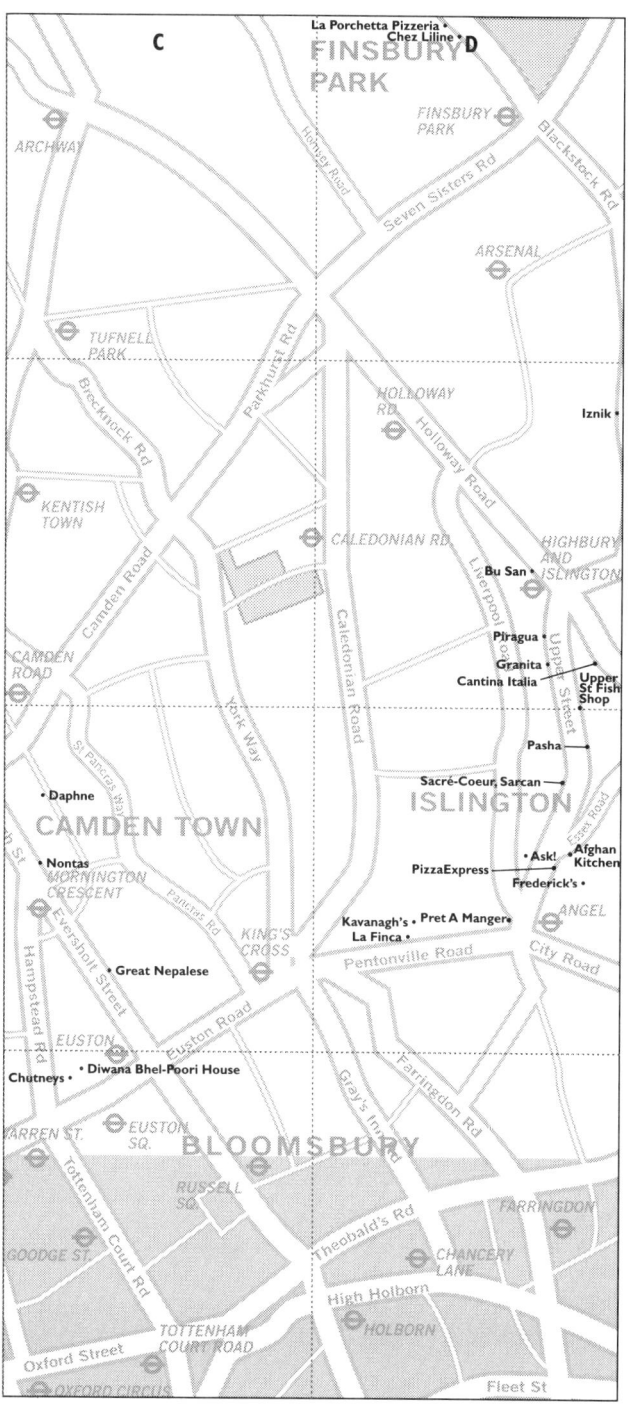

MAP 9 – THE CITY

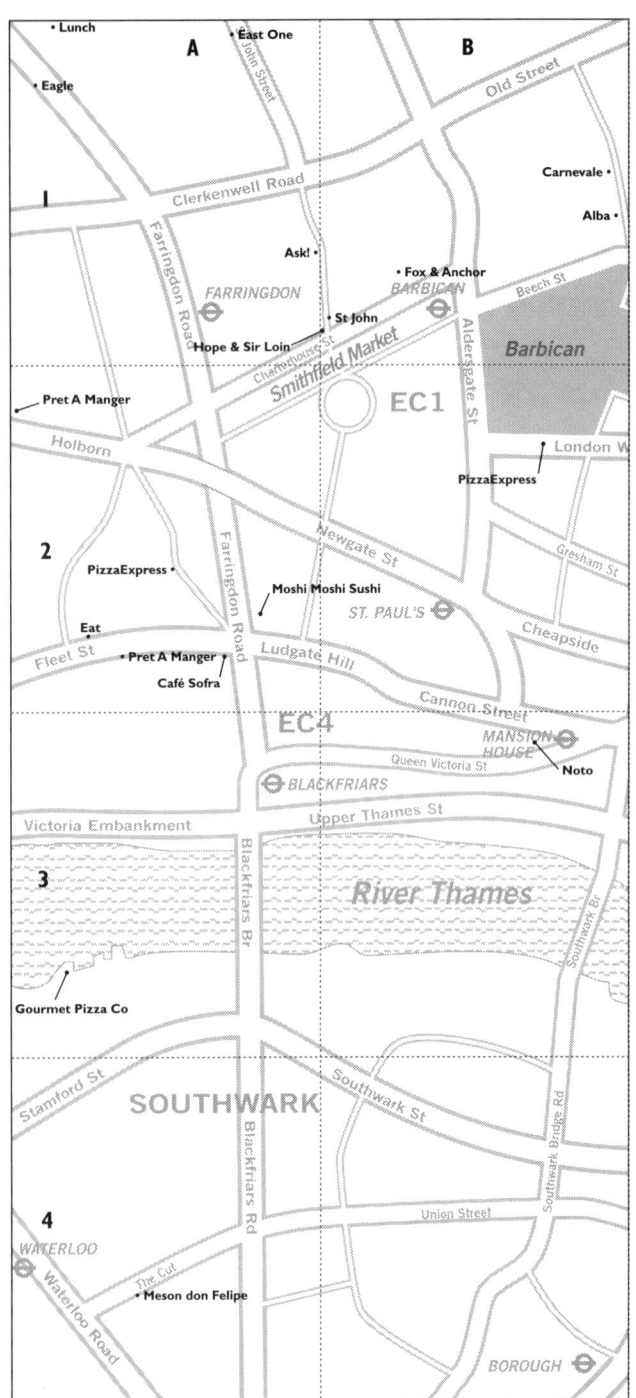

MAP 9 – THE CITY

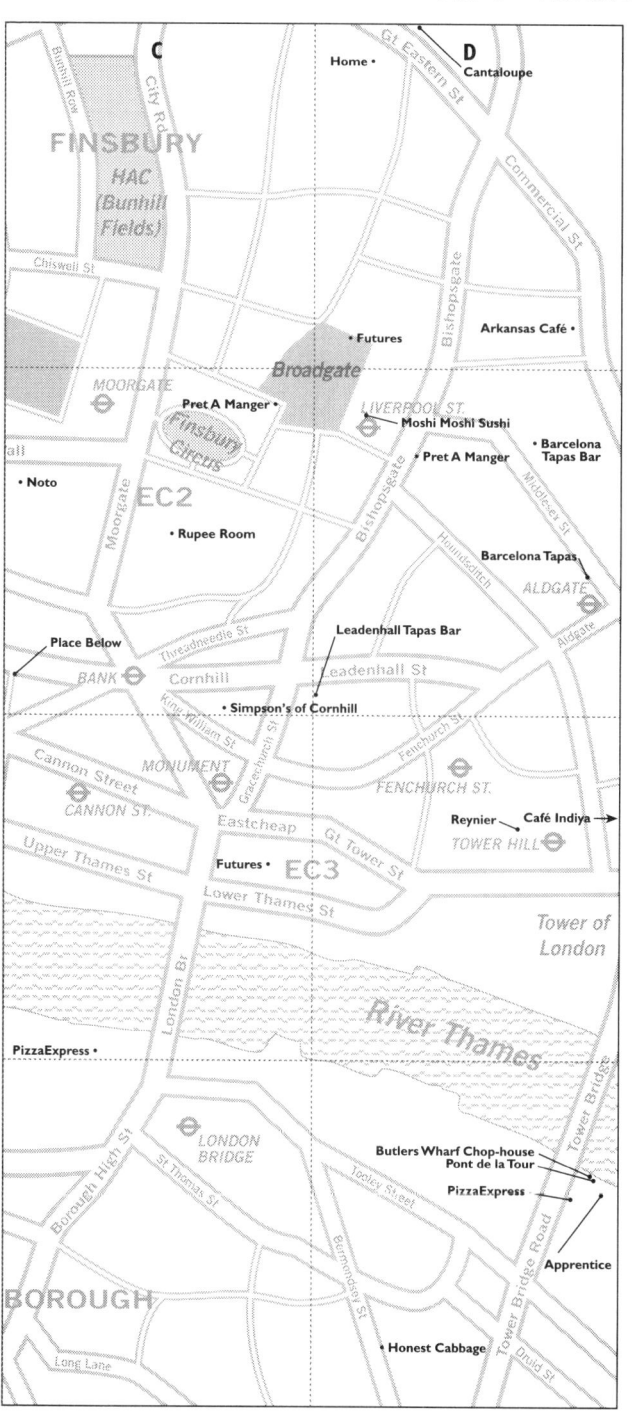

MAP 10 – SOUTH LONDON (AND FULHAM)

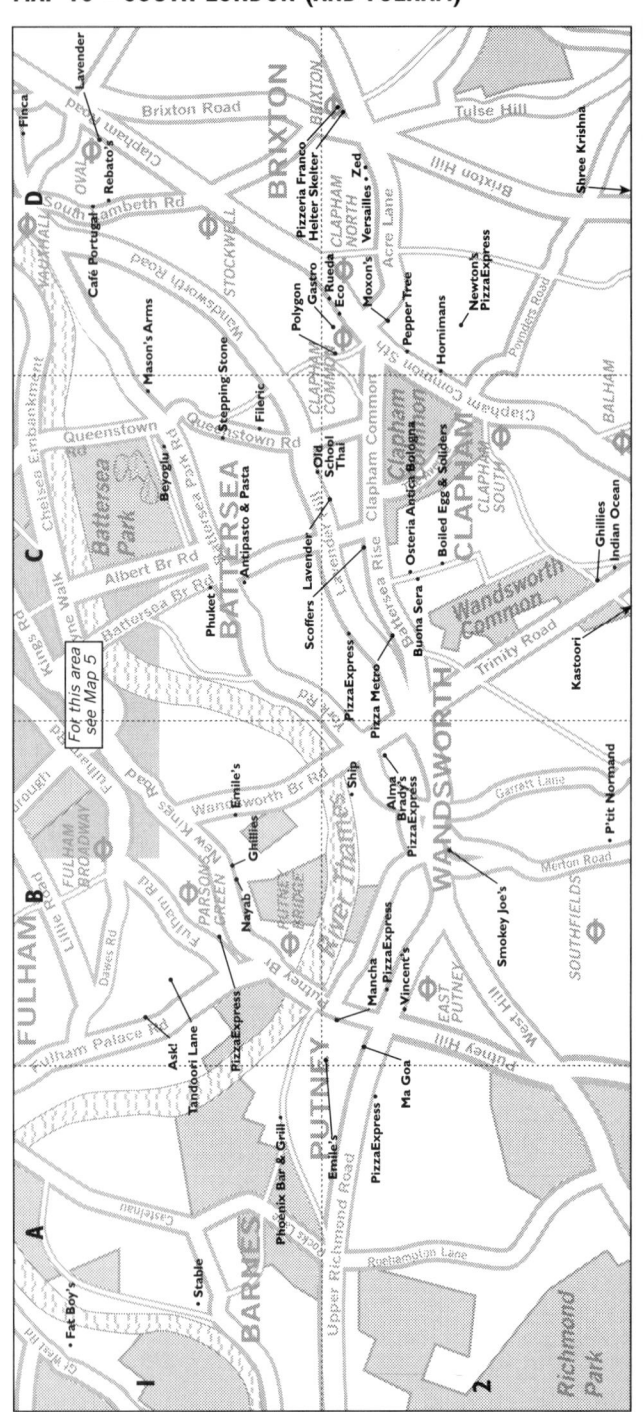

NOTES

NOTES

NOTES

NOTES

NOTES

NOTES